# Cooperative
# Grouping
# for
# Interactive
# Learning

**The Authors**

Lawrence Lyman is Associate Professor, The Teachers College, Emporia State University, Kansas.

Harvey C. Foyle is Assistant Professor of Education, Emporia State University, Kansas.


**The Advisory Panel**

Sharon Rose Bell, Elementary Teacher, James Monroe Elementary School, Manitowoc, Wisconsin

Joseph P. Caliguri, Professor and Chair, Division of Educational Administration, University of Missouri-Kansas City

Marge Harris, Social Studies Teacher, Martha's Vineyard High School, Massachusetts

Sandra J. Leder, Calcasieu Parish Schools, Lake Charles, Louisiana

Tedd Levy, Social Studies Teacher, Norwalk Public Schools, Connecticut

Edna Henry Rivers, High School Counselor, W. P. Davidson High School, Mobile Alabama

Dan Smith, Department Chair, Special Education, South Hadley High School, Massachusetts

**NEA**
**SCHOOL RESTRUCTURING SERIES**

# Cooperative Grouping for Interactive Learning:
## Students, Teachers, and Administrators

**Lawrence Lyman**
**and**
**Harvey C. Foyle**

*Robert McClure*
*NEA Mastery In Learning Project*
*Series Editor*

nea PROFEJIONAL LIBRARY
National Education Association
Washington, D.C.

## Acknowledgment

The authors would like to thank the many teachers and administrators from our classes and in-service workshops whose enthusiasm, energy, and dedication serve as a constant source of ideas and inspiration to us.

We would like to especially recognize the following people for their collegiality and support: Daryl Berry, Joanne Foyle, Susan Lyman, Mike Morehead, Jack Skillett, and Gene Werner.

—Lawrence Lyman
Harvey C. Foyle

**Printing History**
   **First Printing:**    **August 1990**
   **Second Printing:**  **September 1991**

## Note

The opinions expressed in this publication should not be construed as representing the policy or position of the National Education Association. Materials published by the NEA Professional Library are intended to be discussion documents for teachers who are concerned with specialized interests of the profession.

**Library of Congress Cataloging-in-Publication Data**

Lyman, Lawrence.
   Cooperative grouping for interactive learning / by Lawrence Lyman and Harvey C. Foyle.
      p.    cm.
   Includes bibliographical references.
   ISBN 0-8106-1842-7
   1. Communication in education.    I. Foyle, Harvey Charles.
II. NEA Professional Library (Association)    III. National Education Association of the United States.    IV. Title.
LB1033.5.L95   1990
371.1'02—dc20                    90-37337
                                           CIP

# CONTENTS

# INTRODUCTION: SCHOOL IMPROVEMENT THROUGH COLLEAGUESHIP AND COOPERATION

*The highest and best form of efficiency is the
spontaneous cooperation of a free people.* *

To maintain and build quality, schools, like all other complex institutions, require the cooperation of free people. Of the vast amount of writing that has appeared in the last several years on improving schools, little has touched on how the people responsible for them can develop better relationships, new forms of colleagueship, or new ways for working together more productively. Little has been written of the practical considerations for reforming schools from the inside.

This is, perhaps, only right and proper since the early stages of the movement for reform required the testing of new visions, the creation of conceptual underpinnings, and the development of a research orientation to generate new kinds of knowledge and ways of acquiring that knowledge. The first book in the NEA School Restructuring Series, *Teachers and Research in Action*, attempted to provide a fresh view of what knowledge we need to improve our schools and how practitioners and researchers could work together to produce those understandings. In subsequent books, we will return occasionally to topics on the underlying substantive features of school improvement. The major interest in the NEA School Restructuring Series, however, is to help teachers, principals, and other faculty members with the demanding and complex job of fundamentally improving their schools. *Cooperative Grouping for Interactive Learning: Students, Teachers, and Administrators* provides such assistance.

Three aphorisms describe the phenomenon of faculty-led school improvement. The first, according to teachers, is *we are taking a trip without a roadmap*; there are no rules, little precedence, only the clarity and strength of the group's vision to guide the school community to its destination.

---

Bernard Baruch, *American Industry at War: A Report of the War Industries Board*, Washington, D.C.: U.S. Government Printing Office, 1921.

The second aphorism teachers involved in school improvement work cite is *we are rebuilding the airplane while it's in flight*. Business and other institutions can often be "closed for remodeling," but this is not the case with schools. (Although it requires great time and energy to keep a school going and improve it at the same time, it is likely that the effort will be better than if the school were closed during the improvement period. The result is more relevant to those who benefit from the improvement, more easily and effectively implemented by those responsible for the change.)

Finally, school-based, faculty-led reformers have discovered the old newspaper editor's adage, *if it's not local, it's not real*. Top-down approaches to improving schools, which characterized many of the early reform efforts of the early eighties, have now been replaced with greater attention to the needs of individual learning communities.

This book addresses these three concerns with originality, clarity, and concreteness. Through text and a great number of activities and exercises, the authors help faculties to develop a way of thinking about themselves and to use those insights in their improvement efforts. The materials in these chapters are thoroughly grounded in what is known about adult learning and can spark the interests of even the most diffident group.

Similarly, the material developed for both younger and older students is developmentally appropriate. The various activities described in these chapters will foster positive interaction among students in their classrooms and in the broader school community. Students are seen in this book as important contributors to the renewal effort, not just the benefactors of reform.

True restructuring of our schools grows from a foundation of solid content, good pedagogy, and an environment made up of people who are inquiring, supportive and respectful of one another. This book will help school people build and maintain such a culture.

—Robert M. McClure, Director
NEA Mastery In Learning Project

# 1. RESTRUCTURING WITHOUT REBUILDING

The decade of the 1980s can be appropriately labeled the "decade of reform." Beginning with *Nation at Risk*, the report released in 1983 by the Carnegie Foundation, a chorus of calls for reform and restructuring of the schools has been heard. These reform reports share the consensus that American education must make changes in order to meet the needs of students who will attend school in the 1990s. The need for change has been clearly established. It is time to make an effective response to the needs of students that have been so clearly identified.[1]* The current literature would suggest that the 1990s may well be a decade of restructuring.[2] Whether that restructuring helps to make the schools more or less effective in meeting the changing needs of their clientele remains to be seen.

To restructure our schools, school buildings do not need to be rebuilt. Schoolrooms do not need to be remodeled. Teachers do not need to be replaced. Indeed, the financial costs of such efforts are clearly beyond the means and will of the federal government and most state governments. If effective and lasting restructuring is to take place, it must come from within the school buildings and not from outside. Change must be managed by those most intimately and directly concerned with the students whose needs have made restructuring so pressing. Government mandate cannot force lasting change.

Educators must begin to talk with each other about those methods of teaching and administrating schools that have clearly been identified as effective in meeting the academic and affective needs of students. One such methodology is cooperative learning. Numerous studies have established the effectiveness of cooperative learning as a strategy to increase the academic achievement of students while meeting their affective needs and increasing their liking of school.[3] While cooperative learning is in use in many schools and classrooms, its use is not as widespread as its effectiveness would dictate. It is unrealistic to expect that the benefits of cooperative learning can be fully realized in a nonsupportive environment. As teaching methodology changes, so must the classroom environment.

---

*Superior numbers appearing in the text refer to the Notes at the end of the chapter.

# RESTRUCTURING THE ROLE OF THE ADMINISTRATOR

In 1988, the Carnegie Foundation released a report examining the state of the schools from the perspective of 13,500 teacher respondents.[4] At the same time as teachers are being held increasingly accountable for student progress in school, they also feel relatively powerless to make changes in the conditions of their classrooms and schools. One particularly alarming finding of the report was that teachers encounter more "red tape and bureaucracy" than in the past. Ernest Boyer, author of the report, gives the reform movement a failing grade in improving the conditions of teachers.

Administrator relationships with teachers are too often evaluative, coercive, and judgmental. Many teachers dread a visit from the principal in the same way that many students hate to go back to school in the fall. They know they will be judged and found wanting. Most principals seek a positive relationship with their teachers, but the structure of their school district, in which power is hoarded at the central office and decisions affecting the school directly are made by those outside the building, limits their effectiveness in interacting in a positive manner with teachers.

If meaningful restructuring is to take place, therefore, the board of education and central office administration of the school district must play a key role. The board and central office administration must be willing to share their power and allow participation in appropriate decisions. These relationships must be worked out in collaboration with the building administrative staff and the teaching staff in each individual attendance center and may necessarily be different depending on the needs of the particular school.[5]

Teachers must be given the opportunity to become directly and meaningfully involved in decisions that affect them and the students they teach. Because teachers are most directly and intimately involved with the day-to-day lives of students, they can have the most immediate and lasting effect on student achievement and attitude. When teachers are given reasonable freedom to think about the structure of their classrooms, to change student grouping patterns, and to revise instructional patterns, for example, they can experience the "exhilaration" of taking control of their teaching.[6]

# RESTRUCTURING TEACHER INTERACTIONS

Teachers find themselves isolated from their peers by logistics, time, and tradition.[7] The necessary time for collaborative planning, shared decision making, peer coaching, skills training, and other necessary interactions is simply not found in many schools. Staff development sessions often involve little teacher interaction. Too many teachers in America end their teaching day lonely and frustrated. This frustration may be exacting a high price in lowered teacher morale, reluctance of new candidates to enter the profession, and burnout. Teacher isolation denies teachers the support team that is crucial to their success, impedes collaboration, and stands as a barrier to true restructuring of the schools.[8]

## RESTRUCTURING AND THE STUDENT

Too many students in America go to school in a traditional, lonely classroom where they are isolated from their peers and taught to learn in silence. Too often, spontaneity and student interaction are punished rather than rewarded. Such learning environments prove especially frustrating for those whose socioeconomic background, academic readiness, learning style, and motivation to learn make achievement in such an environment difficult or impossible. Student isolation also frustrates the social needs of students.[9]

Every student must take responsibility for his or her own individual learning. At the same time, students must also be encouraged to take responsibility for the success of other students in the classroom. This is hardly a new idea—students in one-room schools learned this way throughout America in the early part of this century. In the restructured classroom of the 1990s, student interaction and cooperation can form the base for improved problem solving, increased achievement, better retention of material, and better attitudes toward school, subject, teachers, and peers.

## WHAT IS NEEDED

In order to begin the process of restructuring, or to continue restructuring efforts already underway, school personnel must recognize that a crisis exists that threatens the long-term effectiveness and credibility of our schools. Those who would restructure our schools must be willing to admit that traditional, top-down structures in our schools have failed to involve large numbers of students in productive learning.

For many students, schools have failed to nurture positive self-esteem and attitudes. Too many students have left school without the basic skills needed for successful participation in our society. That the schools are not solely or even primarily responsible for these failures may be argued. However, these highly publicized failures have created a crisis of public confidence in the schools of such severity that it may not be too dramatic to say that the very survival of our schools rests on the abilities of educators to make the changes in structure and practice necessary to involve significantly more students productively in the educational process.

A logical place to consider restructuring efforts would be in the colleges and universities that prepare teachers and principals. It is lamentable that there are still colleges of education that graduate teachers and principals who are not equipped with the skills necessary for effective collaboration and cooperation. Interactive teaching methods must find their way into the college classrooms where education personnel are prepared, and the skills necessary for effective interaction should be a part of every education preparation program.

Restructuring must also involve classified personnel, parents, and the community. Parent involvement in appropriate decision-making processes of the school needs to be encouraged and nurtured. A positive trend in community involvement is the school-business partnership that some schools have been able to facilitate. Adopt-a-school programs encourage positive interaction between industry and the students who will be the workers of the future. Such efforts must be expanded.[10] Structuring a positive classroom environment for students will necessitate the involvement of all who work with students and those with a stake in their futures.

While the involvement of universities and those who work with students in nonteaching roles is necessary, the individual attendance center is the most appropriate nucleus for productive change. Teachers and principals must be seen as the agents and facilitators of the necessary changes that will need to take place, not as enemies of or impediments to those changes. Teachers and principals must also work as allies, not adversaries, to bring about appropriate changes. Decentralization of power and decision making is needed so that schools can experiment with change, interact with students, and measure the results. Only then can teachers and principals be realistically held accountable for student progress.

The success of any restructuring effort is dependent on the degree and amount of group-building activities that take place prior to and during the restructuring activities. Barriers to working together need to be overcome, suspicion and distrust reduced, and collegiality built. Group-building activities promote trust, foster cohesion and mutual acceptance, and provide the foundation on which successful collaborative efforts can be built. While time consuming, they cannot be ignored if meaningful, lasting change is to take place.

A critical factor in the success of any restructuring effort is time. Time must be given to plan, analyze, and decide what is best for every attendance center. Teachers need opportunities to plan together, to assess achievement data, to share successes, and to work to remediate failures. Time must also be given to acquire the skills necessary for teachers and principals to interact effectively with students and with each other. To find such time, administrators must be willing to streamline procedures, reduce unnecessary paperwork, and eliminate nonessential meetings.

Individuals, no matter how skilled, do not necessarily bring the skills and attitudes needed for successful participation in the restructured school. Those who advocate change must be willing to make the effort necessary to build the groups. Group building requires that group members feel comfortable working together. The skills needed to participate successfully in group work also have to be acquired. Opportunities to practice newly learned skills in decision making are also essential components of the restructuring process.

What should be the desired outcomes of these restructured efforts? Restructuring should promote cooperation among administrators, teachers, and students. School personnel should function as a team to achieve agreed-on goals. Teachers should be directly involved in the budget, curricular, assessment, and planning decisions that affect them and the students they teach.

In the classroom, restructuring would promote and nurture cooperative learning processes which have been shown by research to be highly effective when appropriately implemented. While cooperative learning is not the only desirable strategy for teaching, it should form a part of every student's instructional experience. Students should have regular opportunities to work as part of a team, and to experience the satisfaction of contributing to the team's success.

In the classroom of the 1990s, high expectations for the academic success of virtually all students can become realistic. As students learn to work together as a group, they can form support teams, tutorial relationships, and informal networks to maximize learning effectiveness. The success of the class in working together becomes an important factor in assessing the progress of the students.

As technological change expands the base of information available to teachers and students, the teacher's role in the classroom must also expand and change to facilitate increased student learning. Teachers can become involved in teaching the processes of information location, assessment, and problem solving. As students become more adept and creative in working together to learn, opportunities for learning expand so that even classroom conflict can provide opportunities for further learning.

## CONCLUSION

Restructuring the schools appears to be the only way that schools can meet the challenges presented to them by the diverse students who will attend school in the 1990s. Such restructuring need not take large outpourings of money, nor do massive personnel changes need to be made. Commitment to restructuring will require that teachers and principals learn to collaborate effectively to make site-based decisions for the needs of their students. Such a commitment necessitates empowerment from the governing bodies and administrators of school districts, as well as a fundamental change in the way teachers are viewed and in the way teachers view themselves. New attention must be given to fostering the dynamics of group functioning and to building an environment in which research-proven teaching methodologies that foster positive student interaction can flourish. As teachers become less isolated and students become more fulfilled, the current concerns about student achievement can be productively addressed.

## NOTES

1. A discussion of the reform movements by noted educational leaders can be found in Beatrice Gross and Ronald Gross, eds., *The Great American School Debate: Which Way for American Education?* (New York: Simon and Schuster, 1986). A summary of the major reform reports and their findings can be found in Max Heim et al., *The Superintendent and the School Board: The Call for Excellence* (Manhattan, Kans.: The Master Teacher, 1989), Appendix B.

2. A comprehensive discussion of restructuring can be found in Anne Lewis, *Restructuring American Schools* (Arlington, Va.: American Association of School Administrators, 1989). A useful guide to reorganization is found in Jerry Patterson et al., *Productive School Systems for a Nonrational World* (Alexandria, Va.: Association for Supervision and Curriculum Development, 1986).

3. See, for example, Robert Slavin, *Cooperative Learning: Theory, Research, and Practice* (Englewood Cliffs, N.J.: Prentice Hall, 1990). The bibliography at the end of this book includes many other resources that discuss the research on cooperative learning.

4. Ernest L. Boyer, *Report Card on School Reform: The Teachers Speak* (Princeton, N.J.: Carnegie Foundation for the Advancement of Teaching, 1988).

5. A discussion of the need for site-based management can be found in American Association of School Administrators, *School-Based Management: A Strategy for Better Learning* (Arlington, Va.: American Association of School Administrators, 1988).

6. Charles Thompson, "Knowledge, Power, Professionalism, and Human Agency," in *Teachers and Research in Action*, Carol Livingston and Shari Castle, eds., p. 91 (Washington, D.C.: National Education Association, 1989).

7. The need for teacher empowerment and improvement of the status of teachers is discussed in Gene I. Maeroff, *The Empowerment of Teachers: Overcoming the Crisis of Confidence* (New York: Teachers College Press, 1988). Teacher frustrations with their relationships with administrators are discussed in James Herndon, *Notes from a Schoolteacher* (New York: Simon and Schuster, 1985) and Patrick Welsh, *Tales Out of School: A Teacher's Candid Account from the Front Lines of the American High School Today* (New York: Viking, 1986). William Glasser proposes a change in the way teachers view themselves in *Control Theory in the Classroom* (New York: Harper and Row, 1986).

8. Maeroff's book (see note 7) also discusses the problem of teacher isolation. John Goodlad has documented this problem in *A Place Called School: Prospects for the Future* (New York: McGraw-Hill, 1984).

9. The characteristics and needs of at-risk students are analyzed in Judy Brown Lehr and Hazel Wiggins Harris, *At-Risk, Low-Achieving Students in the Classroom* (Washington, D.C.: National Education Association, 1988). William Glasser discusses the problem of student frustration and the growing numbers of students not working to their potential in *Control Theory in the Classroom* (see note 7). Arthur Powell, "Being Unspecial in the Shopping Mall High School," *Kappan* 67, no. 4 (December 1985): 255–261, discusses how easily adolescents can be "lost" in the structures of many current schools.

10. Adopt-a-school programs are discussed in Story Moorefield, "The Burgeoning Adopt-a-School Movement," *Streamlined Seminar* (National Association of Elementary School Principals) 7, no. 2 (November 1988). Ways for businesses to become productively involved in school restructuring are outlined in National Alliance of Business, *A Blueprint for Business on Restructuring Education* (Washington, D.C.: National Alliance of Business, 1989).

# 2. GROUP BUILDING FOR POSITIVE INTERACTION

Teachers and administrators can restructure their classrooms and schools to encourage cooperation. However, many students and teachers have had limited opportunities to work together. Students and teachers do not necessarily have the attitudes and motivation to work together with others to accomplish group tasks. The most important initial factor for building a positive environment in the school and in the classroom is group building.[1] *Group building* is the process of creating a cohesive group that functions positively and productively to accomplish tasks.

## THE NEED FOR GROUP BUILDING

The student comes to a new classroom as a stranger. He or she may quickly recognize old friends and gravitate toward them or may remain isolated. Students tend to bond together with those they perceive to be the same as they are. When the teacher does not work to make each member feel part of the group, students do not always choose to meet those members of the class who seem different. Or the other members of the class may choose to ignore a new member or make a student a scapegoat for the problems of a group or the class as a whole. In this way, cliques are formed, and those who do not belong are further isolated.

When individual class members do not feel comfortable with each other, it is difficult for them to participate successfully in cooperative learning activities, even if the activities themselves are well designed and appropriate. Discipline problems are common in such settings, as are complaints that individual group members are "not doing their part." Some teachers give up trying to use cooperative methods because of the strain such problems cause.

To some extent, new teachers also come to their schools as strangers. Beyond well-intentioned "buddy systems" that are usually informal and of short duration, many administrators have made little effort to induct their new teachers into the group. Some groups of teachers who have worked together for years have never come together as a team. They work as isolated individuals behind their classroom doors or in informal groups or cliques with other teachers with whom they feel comfortable and compatible. Interpersonal relationships between teachers are too often strained, with long-standing jealousies and prejudices about other faculty members all too common.

When adults who do not feel comfortable with each other are asked to collaborate and become involved in sharing power, communication is often difficult. Progress is slow because individual group members may not be committed to the success of others in the group. More assertive teachers may dominate their groups, with the good ideas of less assertive teachers unspoken or ignored. A "let's get this over with" attitude may prevail, causing the products of group activities to be disappointing and not representative of the total group.

Group building involves students, teachers, or administrators in planned activities that embody the requirements of successful cooperative learning. Because group builders are designed so that participants experience success, positive attitudes are nurtured and a foundation for further successful cooperation is built. In order to promote and sustain successful collaboration and cooperation, group-building activities are necessary at the beginning and throughout a group's working relationship.

As they work together on group-building tasks, group members develop an appreciation for the differences individuals bring to the group. These differences may include personality traits, experiences, socioeconomic differences, cultural differences, religious differences, and gender differences. Group members can learn how different priorities and values, different skills and aptitudes, and different problem-solving approaches can assist the group as it works together. Group building also enhances individual self-esteem as the group members see their contributions are of value and their ideas are worthwhile to the group. This encourages individuals who might not usually contribute in group settings to do so.

## GROUPING FOR GROUP-BUILDING ACTIVITIES

Group-building activities take place in heterogeneous groups of two to six people. Group size is determined by the nature of the group-building activity. Smaller group size is usually more successful when group builders are used with less experienced individuals.

One of the purposes of group builders is to bring together people who would not necessarily choose to work together. They are then given a common task with a high probability of success. The classroom teacher, for example, would find it helpful to give each student the chance to work with every other student in class during the first weeks of school. For the adult leader, the goal would be a similar one: to promote positive interaction among all of the people who work together as a group.

The leader may group participants in group-building activities randomly. This can be done by counting off members, grouping according to colors worn, or countless other random methods. This random method is appropriate if a tally is kept to assure that all members of the larger group work in a small group with every member at some time.

To promote heterogeneity, group members may also be selected according to factors such as sex, ethnicity, socioeconomic background, cultural background, or achievement. In the classroom, the teacher who structures groups using such criteria tries to make each group somewhat representative of the class as a whole. For example, if the class has an equal number of males and females, each small group would also. If the class has an ethnic group representing about a fourth of the class as a whole, each small four-person group would have a member from the ethnic group.

Teachers may be grouped for group building activities by making sure each group has different grade levels or subject areas represented. It may be productive to make sure that each group has males and females if the faculty membership permits it. Remember, the goal of grouping students or teachers is to get people together who would not otherwise necessarily work together.

## POSITIVE GROUP INTERDEPENDENCE

Group-building activities are structured so that the group members must depend on each other to successfully complete the task. Positive interdependence among group members while completing group-building activities accustoms individuals to working together with others. As the groups are working together, the leader needs to monitor the groups to make sure all are involved in the task.

Some group-building activities use group roles to make sure that all the members are involved and make a positive contribution to the group's effort. Some common roles include facilitator (keeps the group moving and makes sure all participate), writer (writes down the group's ideas), and encourager (says positive things about group members). Roles should be suited to the requirements of the group. The names and functions of the roles change as the objectives and outcomes of the group builder dictate.[2]

## GROUP REWARD

Group-building activities include a group reward; that is, something desired by the members of the group happens as a result of the group's successful completion of the group-building task. When group-building tasks are designed so that they are challenging and fun, the group re-

18

ward can often be the simple enjoyment derived from working together on a motivating activity. The support and approval of other members in the group is often the only reward adult groups need. Tangible rewards, praise from the administrator, or the sharing of the successful results of group activities with other groups can also be appropriate group rewards for group builders used with adults.

External group rewards for students may include posting the names of groups that successfully completed the task on a chart, chalkboard, or bulletin board. Tangible rewards such as stickers, certificates, small prizes, or appropriate food can also be used. If the group-building activity was genuinely enjoyable for the students, however, no other reward may be needed.

Success is an important aspect of the group reward. The group-building activity must be designed to promote a high degree of success for all group members. It is important to make sure that the activity is designed so that all group members can make a contribution to the group effort. This is accomplished by using a variety of content, categories, and other elements that appeal to interests and abilities of each individual within the group.

Competition between groups should be carefully considered as it may prove counterproductive to the overall goal of building cooperation and mutual regard. Competition for group rewards can encourage cheating. Scapegoating, blaming one individual for the group's failure, can also occur. Competition between groups can cause members of nonwinning groups to feel unsuccessful and reluctant to work cooperatively in future tasks.

Debriefing after the activity is important so that participants in group-building activities have an opportunity to verbalize their feelings about working together in the group. This can be accomplished by having individual group members tell their groups what they enjoyed about working together or by sharing positive results from groups with the whole group.

## INDIVIDUAL ACCOUNTABILITY

Individuals must also be responsible for learning from their participation in group-building activities. Individual progress can be measured in a variety of ways. The leader may ask each individual to write down one thing he or she learned from the group-building experience. Participants may be asked to generate another example relevant to the group builder. Another way to measure individual learning is to ask participants to apply the learning to themselves: "How would you use this idea?" The feelings of group members may be measured by asking "What did you enjoy about the activity?"

19

Grading of student group-building activities is almost always inappropriate. The purpose of the group builder is to have the team work together and to have the group-building experience generate positive attitudes. Group grading, if used at all, should be incorporated only after the purpose of working together is clear to students and they have shown skill in cooperating. Premature or inappropriate use of group grading can cause student and parental anxiety and interfere with the implementation of cooperative activities in the classroom.

## ANALYZING THE ELEMENTS OF A GROUP-BUILDING ACTIVITY

The following activity is designed to be used with a wide variety of audiences. Notice each of the elements of a group builder that is present in the example.

### Four in a Row

*Objectives:*
1. Given a list of characteristics, group members will identify the characteristics that apply to them and to other members of their group.
2. Participants will appreciate the qualities of other group members.
3. Participants will experience success by contributing to the group effort.

*Materials:*
One activity sheet per group (see Figure 2–1)
One writing instrument per group

*Procedure:*
Members of the large group are regrouped by the leader into groups of four. Three-member groups are acceptable if the group does not divide evenly into four. Groups are to read each characteristic and write the names of group members to which the characteristic applies in the square. The goal is to have a line of four squares—up and down, across, or diagonal—in which the name of at least one group member is written.

1. The group builder involves *heterogeneous grouping*. Groups are organized by criteria determined in advance by the leader.

2. The group builder promotes *positive interdependence* among group members. It is unlikely that any single member could fill four adjoining squares without using other group members' names as well. The

20

## Figure 2-1
## Four in a Row

| | | | |
|---|---|---|---|
| eaten food from a fast food restaurant | driven or ridden in a car with four doors | trimmed your fingernails or toenails | talked with your brother or sister |
| chewed a piece of sugarless gum | watched a sporting event on TV | petted a dog or cat | played a musical instrument |
| attended church or a religious class | recycled an aluminum can | played a computer game | read at least one chapter of a fiction book |
| drawn or doodled on a piece of paper | visited a shopping mall or center | ridden a bicycle or exercise bicycle | worn a shirt or sweatshirt with words on it |

use of a single group sheet and a single writer causes the group to have to work together as well.

3. The *group reward* for the activity can be public recognition of those groups that find four adjoining squares in which one or more names can be written. A food treat could also be used to celebrate the completion of the activity. Items in the squares can be adjusted by the leader so that each group will have a high probability of attaining the group reward.

4. *Individual accountability* can be achieved after the activity. Individuals can be asked to write down two interesting things they learned about other members of their group. Individuals may also be asked to write or tell other group members how they felt about working together in the group. Individuals may be asked to suggest items that could be used for a future Four in a Row activity.

## KINDS OF GROUP BUILDERS

Group-building activities may be used to practice skills needed for successful participation in further group activities. These necessary skills include listening, paraphrasing, resolving conflict, and supporting others. Thinking skills such as creativity, brainstorming, and problem solving are also needed for effective work in groups. Examples of group builders designed to practice particular skills with teachers can be found in Chapters 3 and 4.

In the classroom, group-building activities have six important purposes. *Creative* group builders involve group members in divergent thinking processes. *Critical-thinking* group builders foster problem-solving skills and convergent thinking. *Communication* group builders help students practice oral communication and listening skills as they work with others in the group. *Awareness* group builders help students become aware of the special skills, talents, and perceptions others bring to the group. *Environment* group builders help to promote a caring, positive classroom environment. *Self-esteem* group builders help students build the positive self-concept needed for positive decision making. Examples of each kind of group builder can be found in Chapter 5.

Group builders may also be related to the specific content of a subject area or professional group. For example, a social studies class may work on a geography skill. If content-related group builders are used, the activity should be one with a high probability of success. Any new method or experience can cause anxiety and stress. The leader should be careful that, in the initial stages of group building, anxiety does not become related to the content of the later activities that will be worked on coopera-

22

tively. Many leaders choose to use group builders that are content neutral for this reason.[3]

Group-building activities can be designed for the particular needs and interests of the group. You will notice that many of the group builders included in the following chapters are adaptable to different content areas, interests, and age levels. Statistics from current magazines, ideas from professional journals, and games and puzzles from a wide variety of sources can make up the content of the group builder.

Commercially produced books of activities that can be adapted for group builders are widely available. A suggested list of some of these books can be found in the Selected Bibliography. In evaluating such activities for group builders, the leader should consider whether the activity has a high probability of success and whether each of the elements of a successful group builder can be identified: heterogeneous grouping, positive interdependence, group reward, and individual accountability.

## CONCLUSION

Cooperation and collaboration are often hampered when groups of students and teachers are asked to work together without the use of appropriate group-building activities. Successful group builders incorporate heterogeneous grouping, positive interdependence, group reward, and individual accountability. Success with group-building activities promotes positive feelings among group members and creates a positive climate that encourages further group efforts.

## NOTES

1. Robert Slavin discusses the concept of team building in *Cooperative Learning: Theory, Research, and Practice* (Englewood Cliffs, N.J.: Prentice-Hall, 1990). David Johnson and Roger Johnson have produced a book of warm-up activities for use in conjunction with their cooperative learning training: *Cooperative Learning: Warm-Ups, Grouping Strategies, and Group Activities* (New Brighton, Minn.: Interaction Book Co., 1985).

2. The function of group roles is noted in David Johnson et al., *Circles of Learning: Cooperation in the Classroom* (Alexandria, Va.: Association for Supervision and Curriculum Development, 1984), 30–31.

3. Dee Dishon and Pat Wilson O'Leary give examples of nonacademic cooperative learning activities in *A Guidebook to Cooperative Learning: A Technique for Creating More Effective Schools* (Holmes Beach, Fla.: Learning Publications, Inc., 1984).

# 3. POSITIVE INTERACTION BETWEEN ADMINISTRATORS AND TEACHERS

If meaningful educational change is to be based at the school-building level, the building-level administrator must play a key role in facilitating that change. The principal's interactions with the teachers and students in an individual school building have tremendous impact on the climate of the building—the achievement of individuals within the building, and the morale of all who work there.

Building administrators are expected to assume a variety of roles: as liaisons with the central office, as managers of discipline, as directors of building personnel, as supervisors of buildings and grounds, as directors of student activities, and as public relations coordinators with parents and other community members. Often, the principal finds the role of instructional leader is neglected while fires on other fronts are extinguished.[1]

In order to be effective as leaders of interactive buildings, principals must manage conflicting roles so that sufficient time is available to interact with teachers and students, to reinforce their efforts, and to coordinate and facilitate interaction within the school. To accomplish this task, the principal must be an excellent manager of his or her time.[2] The superintendent, assistant superintendent, and other members of the central office staff must also assist the principal by encouraging the principal to spend a significant part of his or her time in interactions with teachers and students. The central office staff must also be willing to revise their expectations of principals so that these potentially productive interactions can take place.[3]

## INFORMAL INTERACTIONS: A KEY TO POSITIVE CLIMATE

Building principals and assistant principals can make great contributions to the climate of their schools and the morale of teachers and students through simply being visible and willing to interact.[4] The confidence of the teaching staff is a key factor in determining whether teachers will work cooperatively with building administrators. Such confidence is nurtured through frequent positive contacts with the principal and assistant principals. The elements of such contacts include availability, modeling, and reinforcement.

24

As building administrators move out of their offices and circulate through the hallways, classrooms, and lunchrooms of their schools, many opportunities to interact with teachers and students present themselves. The administrator who takes advantage of such opportunities by making himself or herself available to the staff and students can gain insight into and understanding of the problems, concerns, and successes of those in the school. The administrator can also follow up on concerns, when appropriate, and remove some of the minor annoyances that irritate teachers and students as they work together.

An important factor in all informal interactions is modeling. Informal interactions give the administrator a chance to demonstrate, through his or her tone, language, and personal concern, the kind of interactions that are desirable for teachers and students to have with each other. The administrator who is able to maintain a positive tone and demonstrate good listening skills when interacting informally with teachers and students enhances the climate of the school.[5]

When interactions give teachers and students the impression that the administrator is aloof, unconcerned, or negative, the likelihood that teachers will respond to other teachers and students in a similar manner is increased. When adults and children are treated in a caring manner, they are more likely to react that way to others.

Informal interactions also give the administrator the opportunity to reinforce positive behaviors and attitudes of teachers and students. This can be done in several ways:

1. *Showing consideration.* The goal is for the teacher and student to feel that the administrator likes and cares about them. Examples:

   "I know you've been ill. Are you feeling better?"
   "How are you doing in your evening class?"
   "I heard you were elected president of your club. Congratulations."

2. *Showing appreciation.* The goal is for the teacher and student to feel that the supervisor recognizes and values their effort. Examples:

   "Thanks for all your hard work on the project."
   "I appreciate your support."
   "It's such a help to have you here."

3. *Sharing positive remarks.* The goal is for the teacher and the student to know that the administrator is hearing positive things about their performance from others. Examples:

   "Mrs. Smith said your essay was the best one she'd read this semester."

"The principal told me how well the students behaved while you were supervising the playground today."

"John's mother was telling me how pleased she is with how well he gets along with you."

4. *Showing respect.* The goal is for the teacher and student to feel that the supervisor values their professional expertise or their ideas. Examples:

"Before I decide, I wanted to find out what you thought."

"Do you have any suggestions for improving our homework assignments?"

"I'd like you to work with that difficult group. I know you can handle them."

Because of the importance of frequent positive contacts with staff, administrators may want to keep a record to assure they are visiting with all teachers on a regular basis. A simple chart can show which teachers have not been visited recently, and the administrator can make sure contacts are made equitably.

## BUILDING TEACHER TRUST AND CONFIDENCE IN THE ADMINISTRATOR

In order to build a climate in which teachers feel comfortable in collaborating and sharing decision making, administrators must first win the confidence of the teaching staff.[6] Group-building programs can be organized by the administrator that build teacher trust and encourage collaboration and collegiality in a particular school.

### Group Builder: Sharing Teaching Episodes

*Objectives*:

1. Teachers will identify effective teaching behaviors in a videotaped episode of their administrator teaching a class.
2. Teachers will volunteer to share tapes of their own teaching at future faculty meetings.
3. Teachers will experience success in working on a group activity.

*Procedure*:

The administrator arranges to have a videotape made while teaching a class at the school. It should be a subject with which the administrator feels comfortable. Parental consent for the taping of students and the sharing of the tape should be obtained in advance. At a faculty meeting or in-service session, the administrator shares the tape with teachers. In

26

heterogeneous groups, teachers discuss effective behaviors they observed in the teaching episode. Each group briefly reports on the effective behaviors the members saw.

*Evaluation*:    At the end of the session, each teacher writes a sentence or two telling his or her reactions to the activity. These may be anonymous. Staff members may be ready to volunteer to share videotapes of their own teaching at future faculty meetings. If no volunteers are forthcoming, the administrator can encourage one of the more capable teachers to share.

## INSTRUCTIONAL SUPERVISION

The administrator also makes formal contacts with teachers. These contacts should have three primary criteria if they are to encourage interaction. First, the administrator's contact with the staff should inspire the staff to think creatively, positively, and humanely about the children they work with and the possibilities of change and improvement in those relationships. Second, the administrator's formal contact with the teacher should model the kinds of interaction the administrator wishes to encourage between teachers and between teachers and students. Finally, the administrator should consistently reinforce positive attitudes, behaviors, and accomplishments that have taken place.

As with other aspects of successful interaction, positive supervision and evaluation depend on the extent to which the teacher is prepared for the supervisory interaction. Orientation by the supervisor to the process and goals of supervision and evaluation must take place if evaluation is to be successful. The following group-building activity may help the administrator assess the orientation procedures in his or her building and plan for changes as necessary.[7]

Group Builder: Orientation to Supervision and Evaluation

*Objectives*:   1. Teachers will rate given aspects of the orientation process in the school.
2. Teachers will appreciate the administrator's desire for their participation and input.
3. Teachers will experience success in working on a group activity.

*Materials*:    One rating sheet per group (see Figure 3–1)

*Procedure*:    Teachers are grouped in heterogeneous groups of three or four. They are asked to evaluate the orientation process in the school using the rating sheet below. One sheet is turned in per group. Teachers do not write their names on the group sheet.

## Figure 3–1
## Orientation to Supervision and Evaluation

Your administrators want you to feel comfortable and well informed about the procedures and goals of supervision and evaluation. Discuss the following statements in your group and rate each statement using the items below.

1 = Strongly agree    2 = Agree        3 = Not sure
4 = Disagree         5 = Strongly disagree

1. Orientation to supervision and evaluation is provided for each member of the staff every year.  1 2 3 4 5

2. Orientation activities are completed before classroom observations begin.  1 2 3 4 5

3. The goal of improving the quality of instruction for all students is emphasized as the reason for supervision and evaluation at our school.  1 2 3 4 5

4. We thoroughly understand the procedures that are used by the administrators in making classroom observations.  1 2 3 4 5

5. We know how the administrators will collect data about our classroom and students.  1 2 3 4 5

6. We understand what the conferences following the observation by the administrators in our classrooms will be like.  1 2 3 4 5

7. We have a good understanding of the standards, policies, and procedures for teacher evaluation in our school district.  1 2 3 4 5

8. We have opportunities to ask questions about goals, procedures, and policies for supervision and evaluation.  1 2 3 4 5

9. A pre-conference is held with each teacher before the first observation of the year to make sure each teacher understands the process and to lower teacher anxiety.  1 2 3 4 5

10. New teachers are provided with more intensive orientation activities to familiarize them with supervision and evaluation procedures.  1 2 3 4 5

11. Our administrators follow policies and procedures as outlined during orientation.  1 2 3 4 5

12. Supervision and evaluation at our school are predictable and positive.  1 2 3 4 5

*Individual Accountability:* After the group rating activity, each teacher is asked to write one idea for improving supervision and evaluation in the school. These are submitted anonymously.

The one-on-one interaction between teacher and administrator that takes place in a supervisory conference can be among the most important in improving learning opportunities for students. Such conferences between teachers and administrators are sometimes monologues, dominated by the administrator. Teachers are more likely to make appropriate changes and try new ideas when they are active participants in the conference. Clarification is a technique that helps the supervisor gain information about the teacher, the class, and the rationale for the decisions the teacher is making. Clarification involves asking appropriate questions to involve the teacher in discussing the lesson. These questions should not be perceived by the teacher as a "trap" by which the administrator seeks to gain information to "pounce" on the teacher. Skillful supervisors can use clarification to demonstrate genuine interest in the teacher and assist the teacher in analyzing his or her instructional decisions.[8]

## Group Builder: Clarification

*Objectives*:
1. Teachers will analyze their instruction when asked appropriate questions by the administrator during the post-observation conference.
2. Teachers will actively participate in the conferencing process.
3. Teachers will experience success in working on a group activity.

*Materials*: An anecdotal record of the lesson, made by the supervisor during the observation (This is helpful in planning which clarification questions to use.)

*Procedures*: The administrator asks questions during the conference, so that the teacher is talking at least half of the conference time. The first three questions are generally appropriate for any lesson, since they ask for information that only the teacher can provide.

1. Did the students behave typically during the lesson I observed? If not, what factors made their behavior unusual?
2. What happened before I came into the classroom?
3. What happened after I left the classroom?
4. What topics were you covering in the lesson today? What diagnostic procedures did you use to determine that the objective for the day's lesson was appropriate for the learners?
5. What are you going to do during the next instructional sequence with this group? On what did you base this decision?
6. What aspects of the lesson pleased you?

7. What would you do differently if you were to teach this lesson again?
8. How did you know students understood what you were teaching?
9. How did you make provisions for learners with different needs (learning styles, grouping) during this lesson? Why?
10. How did you encourage positive student interactions during this lesson?

## FACULTY MEETINGS

A regular source of contact between most administrators and their teachers is the faculty meeting. Such interactions offer opportunities to model behaviors that administrators want to encourage teachers to use in the classroom. The faculty meeting also offers an opportunity to build a positive climate.

### Group Builder: Sharing Positive Feelings

*Objectives*:
1. Teachers will share positive feelings about themselves and others with other teachers.
2. Positive teacher feelings about the school will be shared with parents.
3. Teachers will experience success in working on a group activity.

*Materials*: Sheets of paper for each group to record ideas

*Procedure*: Teachers are grouped in heterogeneous groups of three or four. During a faculty meeting, or series of faculty meetings, the administrator reads the incomplete statements below. After each statement is read, each group member completes the statement with something that is true about them. It is not necessary to provide much time for discussion of the positive statements. The goal is for each group member to share something positive. When the last item is read, each group is asked to appoint a recorder to write down the ideas that are stated in the group. Each group member is accountable for having one idea written down on the group sheet, but ideas are turned in anonymously. The administrator makes a copy of all group responses, combining where appropriate if he or she chooses. The completed sheet is shared with the faculty. The principal also sends the list to parents: "Our faculty was discussing what we do well at school. We thought you'd like to see our ideas." This can be sent home as a separate communication or included in the school newsletter.

30

1. One reason my students are lucky to have me as a teacher is
2. Something I really like about teaching is
3. I know I've really helped a student when
4. Something I'm really proud of this year is
5. One thing I tried that really worked well was
6. A student makes my day when he/she
7. One of the best things about my students this year is
8. My principal is really helpful when
9. I know it's all worthwhile when
10. This has been a good week because
11. Something I'm really looking forward to is
12. One thing our school does really well is

The faculty meeting is also an appropriate place to practice skills needed for successful interaction and collaboration. For example, active listening to others is a vital skill for all group activities, regardless of the age level or purpose of the participants. The following group-building activity is designed to help group members learn about each other and identify the individual skills, interests, and talents they may be able to contribute to further group work. Active listening is required of all group members to successfully accomplish the task. This activity has proven successful with students, teachers, and other groups.

## Group Builder: Alike and Different

*Objectives*:
1. Teachers will work together to share information needed to complete the given task.
2. Teachers will appreciate the ways in which other group members are alike and different.
3. Teachers will experience success in working on a group activity.

*Materials*:
One copy of the Alike and Different sheet for each group (see Figure 3-2)

*Procedure*:
Teachers are grouped in heterogeneous groups of three or four. The group's task is to discover ways in which the members of the group are alike and ways in which each individual differs from the others. In the center circle of the flower, a teacher appointed by the group is to write the group's similarities. These will be discovered through conversation and may include such things as these: all members of the small group are married, all were born in the same state, all like chocolate. Anything shared by each

31

member of the group may be used. At least ten things that each member of the small group shares are to be recorded. Each group member is assigned one of the outside circles (or "petals" of the flower). In each outer circle, at least two things about a group member are to be recorded. For example, a group member may be the only male in the small group, or the only grandmother, or the only teacher who has traveled to Europe. Anything unique to an individual in the small group is acceptable. This sharing process may take 15 to 20 minutes.

At the conclusion of the sharing time, each group is asked to circle one interesting or unique thing that was found that all of their group members shared. A teacher (not the one who recorded the answers) from each group shares the thing chosen by the group with the whole group.

*Individual Accountability:* In the small group, each teacher shares how they encourage members of their classes to appreciate each other's similarities and differences.

*Follow-Up Activity:* This activity can be used again at other meetings with different group members. As the group becomes familiar with the activity, it will take less time to share.

## STAFF DEVELOPMENT

If teachers are to be encouraged to promote interaction and cooperation among students, interaction between teachers must also be part of the staff development experiences of teachers. Staff development activities for teachers too often are dominated by "expert talk." Teachers are forced to listen while "experts" they have had little or no say in choosing suggest changes and innovations to be implemented by the teachers. Follow-up activities, if any, are often directed at measuring how the innovations have been implemented, rather than encouraging cooperative planning and further study by teachers and administrators.

Ideally, staff development activities would often have teachers working together in small, heterogeneous groups. Staff development would be planned and developed with considerable teacher input and direction. Opportunities for teachers to get acquainted with each other, to build the group, and to share experiences would be a key part of such programs.

Staff development would also ideally provide teachers with the opportunity to network with other professionals who share their needs. Networks should go beyond the boundaries of the individual school. The central office may be helpful in matching teachers of like interests and

Figure 3-2
Alike and Different

needs. Professional organizations can assist in identifying teachers in other locations who teach in similar subject areas or have similar interests or specialties.[9]

As with group building, staff development should also require individual accountability by helping teachers cooperatively develop realistic individual and group improvement goals. Assistance in formulating improvement goals and then in reaching them would be available from other teachers, administrators, and a network of professionals at other schools. The celebration of success when goals are achieved should be shared by all.[10]

Staff development sessions can also provide opportunities to practice skills needed for successful interaction and collaboration. For example, brainstorming is a crucial skill for group problem solving for adults and students. Successful brainstorming has three goals: fluency, originality, and flexibility. Fluency involves the production of many different ideas. Originality requires that groups think of ideas that are new to them or that are unusual and creative. Flexibility is a higher-level skill that requires groups to generate possible categories for organizing their ideas. The following group-building activity is designed to practice the skills of brainstorming.[11]

### Group Builder: Sticking Together

| | |
|---|---|
| *Objectives*: | 1. Teachers will practice brainstorming in groups. |
| | 2. Teachers will identify ways brainstorming could be used in their classrooms. |
| | 3. Teachers will experience success in working on a group activity. |
| *Materials*: | Two small wood blocks (may be of irregular size) |
| | Sheets of paper for each group to record ideas |
| *Procedure*: | Teachers are grouped in heterogeneous groups of three or four. Given a time limit of five to seven minutes, they are shown the two blocks and asked to think of as many ways as possible that the two blocks could be stuck together temporarily. One teacher in each group is appointed to write down the ideas. This practices fluency, the production of as many ideas as possible. At the end of the time limit, each group counts its ideas and shares the total number produced with the whole group. This provides group recognition of the groups that produced the most ideas and serves as a group reward. |

Given a time limit of five minutes, teachers are asked to choose two ideas they wrote down that were unusual or creative. The goal is to identify ideas that other groups did not come up with. Each group circles two ideas that they believe other groups did not think of. This practices originality, the production of new, unusual, or creative ideas. At the end of the time limit, a teacher from each group (not the same one who previously shared) reads the ideas the group believes are original. Other groups check their own lists, and members raise their hands if they have the idea written down. Groups that thought of ideas other groups did not think of are identified by the leader, and the group recognition serves as a group reward.

To practice flexibility, teachers are asked to group their ideas in as many different categories as they can in ten minutes. Each category must have at least two ideas grouped under it. A group member (not the same one who recorded the ideas earlier) writes down the categories and ideas that fit under the categories. At the end of the time limit, groups can be recognized for fluency by asking groups to share categories they originated. To reward originality, give each group five minutes to circle one category its members believe no other group came up with. Share this information as before, with other groups' members raising their hands if they have the category mentioned written on their sheet.

*Individual Accountability*:   Each group member shares one way brainstorming could be used in his or her class.

*Follow-Up Activity*:   Teachers brainstorm ways the faculty can "stick together." Once collaboration skills are acquired, teachers can use their skills to work on problems of concern to the faculty as a whole. Teachers can also be divided into groups by interest to work on different problems simultaneously. For example, teachers may work in small, heterogeneous groups to brainstorm strategies for working with at-risk students. The strategies listed in Figure 3–3 were the result of collaboration between teachers and administrators at El Dorado (Kansas) Middle School. After the strategies were agreed on, individual teachers could "adopt" an at-risk student from a list provided by the school office. Teachers who "adopted" an at-risk student were required to use the strategies agreed on by the group.[12]

Figure 3-3
Suggestions for Working with At-Risk Students

1. Make daily eye contact with the students. Students learn avoidance skills early, so breaking down this resistance may take time.

2. Make daily verbal contact with the students. Call the students by name and speak to them whenever you see them.

3. Greet the students by name and tell them goodbye when they leave. Students with attendance problems do respond to being told "I will see you tomorrow."

4. Provide tutoring. Occasionally be willing to inconvenience yourself to give extra academic help to a student.

5. Offer a ride home on occasion if you are comfortable with this. Many at-risk students are latch-key.

6. Encourage students to participate in an extracurricular activity.

7. Attend a school activity in which these students participate. Students notice if you support their programs by your attendance.

8. Write praise and success cards for students. Any improvement in attendance or achievement should receive recognition.

9. Be aware of student achievement in your class and other classes. Check with the counselor at downslip time.

10. Show a genuine concern. It takes teachers who are very secure in their own self-concept to work with these students.

11. Reinforce success by sharing with other teachers so they can say, "I heard that you. . . ." Small successes are most important.

12. Contact parents with positive comments about their students.

13. Check attendance and office referrals. If students are absent, phone home to check.

14. Pay sincere compliments. "Catch 'em being good."

15. Give them a classroom responsibility such as returning books to the library, passing out papers, taking a message to the office, caring for plants—any short-term/no-risk task that is achievable.

16. Give each student 15 minutes one or two times per week.

17. Use cooperative learning strategies. Mixed-ability groups will improve performance of both at-risk and not-at-risk students.

18. Make sure the counselor sees each student on a regular basis, and visit with the counselor yourself.

19. Encourage teachers to adopt an at-risk student in their homeroom.

20. Encourage a peer-tutoring experience for the students.

# CONCLUSION

Administrators' interactions with teachers can inspire teachers to use more cooperative and interactive activities with students. These interactions can also build a positive climate in the school, reduce teacher isolation, and encourage networking and collaboration among teachers.

As the administrators in a school model appropriate interaction with teachers in informal and formal situations, teachers experience the benefits of collaboration and interaction and are encouraged to use these techniques with students. Their efforts can then be reinforced by the administrators.

Informal interactions between teachers and administrators build positive relationships that help the administrators understand the problems and concerns of individual teachers. Having accessible administrators helps to reduce teacher isolation and provides opportunities for reinforcement of the productive behaviors and attitudes that almost all teachers display.

Instructional supervision has great potential for improving the instructional skills of teachers. Instructional supervision is perhaps the most important way in which administrators can influence the achievement, self-concept, and enthusiasm of students. As the productive skills teachers use are identified and encouraged, student achievement becomes more probable, and more positive attitudes are nurtured. Such supervision, however, must be done in a positive, growth-provoking manner that facilitates the active participation of teachers in the process.

Faculty meetings and staff development sessions are more productive when they facilitate active participation rather than passive listening. Activities to get teachers acquainted with each other are appropriate for both faculty meetings and staff development sessions and provide information that may be useful in forming networks among teachers. Practice on the skills needed for collaboration can be done in both settings as well. As teachers become more comfortable with each other and more skilled in collaboration, they can work together to solve problems that confront students, staff, and the organization as a whole with a high probability of success.

# NOTES

1. For a discussion of the role of the principal as instructional leader, see Lawrence Lyman et al., *Clinical Instruction and Supervision for Accountability*, 2d ed. (Dubuque, Iowa: Kendall/Hunt Publishing Co., 1987, Chapter 1). A comprehensive analysis of what makes a principal an effective instructional leader can be found in Wilma F. Smith and Richard Andrews, *Instructional Leadership: How Principals Make a Difference* (Alexandria, Va.: Association for Supervision and Curriculum Development, 1989).

2. Time management for the principal is discussed in Alfred Wilson and Wynona Winn, "The Principal and Time Management," *American Secondary Education* 10, no. 1 (April 1980): 34–39. Another valuable discussion of this topic can be found in "Managing Time for Instructional Leadership," *The Practitioner* (National Association of Secondary School Principals) 15, no. 3 (February 1988): 1–8.

3. Some suggestions for central office administrators to help principals can be found in Lawrence Lyman, "Hey, Central Office, Here's How to Help Principals," *Executive Educator* 9, no. 3 (March 1987): 27–28.

4. See, for example, Dan Cilo, "Principals: Leave Your Offices, Improve Your Schools," *NASSP Bulletin* 73, no. 519 (October 1989): 111–14. Short, "walk through" supervision visits to classrooms are advocated in Madeline Hunter and Doug Russell, *Mastering Coaching and Supervision* (El Segundo, Calif.: TIP Publications, 1989). The benefits of collegiality for teachers and administrators are discussed in Stuart C. Smith and James J. Scott, *Encouraging School Staff to Collaborate for Instructional Effectiveness* (Eugene: Oregon School Study Council, 1989).

5. Useful suggestions for improving the administrator's listening skills are found in Frank Freshour, "Listening Effectively," *Streamlined Seminar* (National Association of Elementary School Principals) 6, no. 2 (November 1987). A method for evaluating the effectiveness of the administrator's listening skills with a rating instrument is provided in Robert Maidment "How Do You Rate Me as a Listener?" *NASSP Bulletin* 71, no. 499 (May 1987): 87–91.

6. The skills needed to build teacher confidence in the administrator are discussed in Lawrence Lyman, Michael Morehead, and Harvey Foyle, "Building Teacher Trust in Supervision and Evaluation," *Illinois School Research and Development* 25, no. 2 (Winter 1989): 54–59. Suggestions for new principals in building staff confidence

and trust can be found in Michael Morehead and Lawrence Lyman, "Three Strategies for New Principals," *Streamlined Seminar* (National Association of Elementary School Principals) 8, no. 3 (January 1990). Guidelines for school climate improvement projects can be found in Eugene Howard et al., the book *Handbook for Conducting School Climate Improvement Projects* (Bloomington, Ind.: Phi Delta Kappa, 1987).

7. Orientation to supervision and evaluation is discussed in Chapter 8 of *Clinical Instruction and Supervision for Accountability* (see note 1). Orientation of teachers is also the focus of a useful ERIC document: Mary Cihak Jensen, *How to Recruit, Select, Induct, and Retain the Very Best Teachers* (Eugene, Ore.: ERIC Clearinghouse on Educational Management, 1987). A practical approach to the orientation of new teachers is discussed in Robert J. Krajewski et al., "Orienting New Staff for Instructional Leadership," *NASSP Bulletin* 72, no. 511 (November 1988): 62–66.

8. Clarification is discussed in Lawrence Lyman and Harvey Foyle, "Creative Supervisory Conferences: New Wine in Old Skins," *Florida ASCD Journal* 6 (Fall 1989): 45–47.

9. The benefits of finding support and assistance from collegial networks is discussed in John Naisbitt and Patricia Aburdene, *Reinventing the Corporation* (New York: Warner Books, 1985), 31–32, 62–63.

10. A comprehensive discussion of productive staff development can be found in Bruce Joyce and Beverly Shower, *Student Achievement Through Staff Development* (New York: Longman, 1988). Needs of adult learners in staff development activities are discussed in Peggy Chnupa Ondrovich, "Staff Development: Meeting Teachers' Psychological and Professional Needs," *ERS Spectrum* 7, no. 4 (Fall 1989): 22–25.

11. Brainstorming is described in the classic Alex Osborn, *Applied Imagination* (New York: Charles Scribner's, 1957). Another excellent source on brainstorming is E. Paul Torrance, *The Search for Satori and Creativity* (Buffalo, N.Y.: Creative Education Foundation, Inc., 1979). The use of brainstorming in instructional supervision conferences is described in "Creative Supervisory Conferences: New Wine in Old Skins?" (see note 8).

12. Thanks to Bonnie Lynch, Merle Patterson, and the teachers of El Dorado (Kansas) Middle School for sharing their ideas.

# 4. POSITIVE INTERACTION AMONG TEACHERS

One of the goals of restructuring the school should be to encourage positive interaction among teachers. Teachers need to work together to plan for change, to solve problems, to help new teachers and students become part of the school, and to help each other improve their instructional skills. Teachers can be of substantial help to each other if they are given the time and encouragement to interact.

A primary barrier to teacher interaction is time. Planning periods are often at different times of the day for teachers who would like to get together. Teachers are often burdened by paperwork and other duties that also restrict their available time to interact with others. Teachers in many schools who wish to interact must do so before or after school hours. Those who have coaching or other extracurricular duties or who take university classes after school find even this time for interaction denied them.

Administrators must be creative in finding time for their teachers to work together. Although dismissal of school for teachers to work together may be unpopular in some communities, a regular time each month could be worked out. Staff development time could also be utilized to provide time for interaction between teachers. Such efforts must be supported by real efforts on the part of administrators to relieve teachers of nonteaching duties and to reduce paperwork and unnecessary meetings.

Group-building activities are also a necessary part of encouraging teachers to work together. Teachers have often worked in isolation and may not recognize the skills and abilities of others. Teachers may be reluctant to share problems or concerns with other teachers with whom they are not comfortable. As group-building activities help teachers to get acquainted and to acquire the needed skills to collaborate effectively, these barriers can be broken down.[1]

## PLANNING FOR CHANGE

Schools need to be restructured to be more responsive to the needs of individual students and teachers. The teachers in a particular school, therefore, must be a part of the planning and implementation of changes that will take place.

An important first step in this process is a needs assessment. Needs assessment is an information-gathering process that identifies strengths and weaknesses of an existing system. Needs assessment is often used to identify deficiencies in the school curriculum, instructional program, or staff. In order to be useful, however, needs assessment must identify both strengths and weaknesses. It is important to know what the school is doing well, so that planned changes will reinforce the strengths.

Needs assessment can involve groups of teachers working together on specific parts of the school program. Outcomes of the school's instructional program are a useful focus for needs assessment in most schools. For example, one group of teachers may analyze test data, looking for both strengths and weaknesses. Teachers at an elementary school may consult with teachers at the middle school their students attend to identify strengths and weaknesses of students as they go to a new school. Another group of teachers may conduct a parent survey to measure parent attitudes and expectations for the school. In high schools, teachers could survey business and community leaders to determine their satisfaction with graduates of the high school. Each needs assessment should be tailored to the particular school and staff.

Another phase of the planning process in some schools is the writing of a philosophy or "mission" statement that embodies the purpose or goal of the school. This statement does not supplant the district philosophy statement if there is one, but serves as a particular statement for an individual school. A philosophy statement for a school is usually short and is phrased to capture the imagination, goals, and ideals of the school. Parents and students may also be involved in the process of discussing what should be in the statement.[2]

Group-building activities can be used to stimulate discussion about the priorities of the school. An activity that shows how relationships between people change in an interactive school follows.

### Group Builder: Organizational Chart

| | |
|---|---|
| *Objectives:* | 1. Teachers will create an organizational chart that shows relationships in the interactive school. |
| | 2. Teachers will appreciate the need for participation by all in an interactive school. |
| | 3. Teachers will experience success in working on a group activity. |
| *Materials:* | One copy of a traditional organizational chart or school district's own chart (Figure 4–1) (optional) |
| | One copy of the blank circular chart (see Figure 4–2) |
| *Procedure:* | Teachers are grouped in heterogeneous groups of three or four teachers. One teacher is appointed to record the |

41

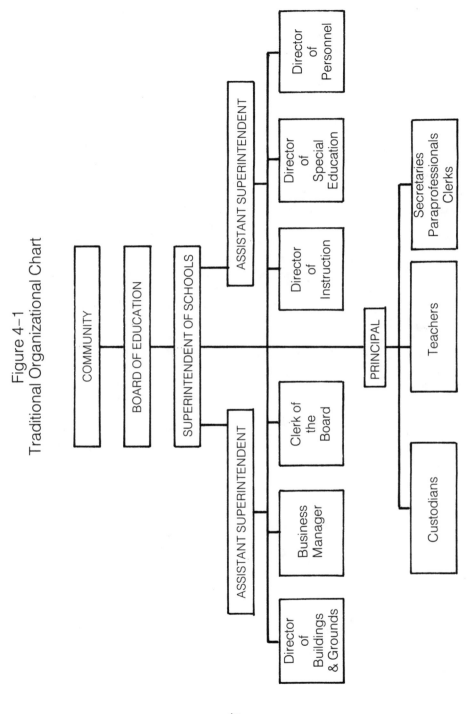

Figure 4–1
Traditional Organizational Chart

# Sample Completed Group Builder

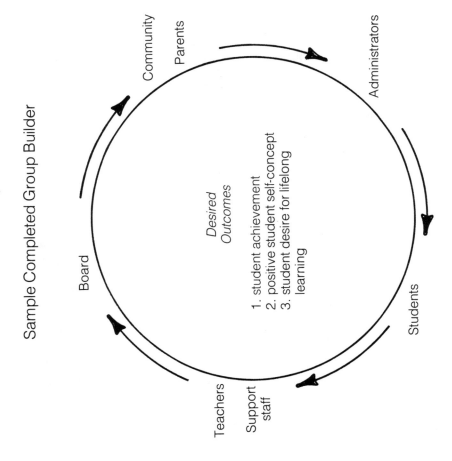

Community
Parents
Administrators
Board
Students
Teachers
Support staff

*Desired*
*Outcomes*

1. student achievement
2. positive student self-concept
3. student desire for lifelong
   learning

group's decisions on the blank circular chart. Each group is given the task of determining the most important priorities of the school. They may have five or fewer responses. The group discussion should center on outcomes that are desired by all in the school. When the group decides on the outcomes they feel are most important for the school, these are recorded in the center circle. After each group finishes, a member of each group (not the teacher who recorded the responses) shares the group's responses with the total group. The leader or an appointed teacher records all responses. Each small group then looks at all responses and is given approximately five minutes to see if any can be combined. The small groups report their findings to the whole group, and statements are combined if the whole group agrees. If there is strong feeling by any individual about keeping a particular response, include it. The final responses chosen by the group are written on an overhead transparency. These can be given to a secretary for typing following the activity.

At the same meeting or a later meeting, each group is again given one copy of the circular chart. If this part of the activity is done at a later meeting, the outcomes decided by the whole group from the first meeting are typed in the center of the circle. On an overhead transparency or chalkboard, the following roles are written: board of education, administrators, teachers, support staff, community, parents, students. Each small group is given the task of arranging these roles around the circle in the spaces between arrows. Since there are more roles than spaces, some will have to be put together (for example, board of education and administrators can be grouped together if the group wishes).

After approximately ten minutes, each group shares its combinations with other groups. Agreement is reached on the best combinations, and they are recorded for typing by the secretary. The leader points out the differences between this organizational chart and the traditional chart: outcomes are at the center of the efforts of those who work in the school, students are included among those who must work to reach the outcomes, no group is more important than another group, all must work together if the outcomes are to be achieved. The completed chart is typed and distributed to faculty and staff. Parents and students may be interested in a copy of the final product as well.

*Individual*
*Accountability:*   Each teacher writes or tells the small group how he or she feels about the new organizational chart.

44

Figure 4–2
Blank Circular Organizational Chart

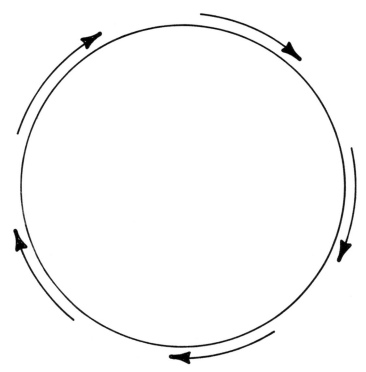

Goal setting is another planning activity that may be collaboratively undertaken by teachers. Short-term and long-term goals may be written that address needs identified in the needs assessment process or during the process of creating the philosophy statement for the school. These goals may be for a single department or grade level or may be school-wide goals. Each goal statement, however, should be reached by consensus of all who will be involved in working toward the goal. Strong commitment of each individual who will work as part of the team is required if goals are to be achieved.

It is important to write both *maintenance* goals and *improvement* goals. Maintenance goals identify areas of current strength in the school that should be recognized and maintained during the change process. Maintenance goals are often neglected, but they serve two important purposes. First, they recognize that the school is already doing some things well. This is important for morale. Second, they guard the unique areas of strength present in each school against changes that may limit their effectiveness.

Improvement goals are more familiar. They specify desired changes that address problems or concerns identified during the needs assessment process. Improvement goals must include desired outcomes: specific, observable criteria that will show that the goal has been achieved.[3]

During these planning processes, the administrator is not a bystander, but facilitates the participation of teachers in the planning activities. The administrator will usually retain "veto" power over elements of planning activities that seem unworkable. Because it is demoralizing to have worked on a plan that is disapproved by higher authority, it is important that teachers be ready to work together. When teachers have the necessary skills and are comfortable in working together, it is unlikely they will create a plan that is totally unacceptable.

A primary function of the administrator in facilitating collaborative planning with teachers, therefore, is to provide instruction in the skills needed to work cooperatively in groups. This may be done during staff development sessions or during faculty meetings. Group-building activities can also be used to practice skills and help the teachers feel comfortable in working together. The planning process will go much more smoothly if teachers have the necessary skills and have participated in group-building activities prior to working on planning activities.

The administrator may also be needed to schedule periods of time and places for meetings, to assist in gathering needed data, and to provide information about how other schools have undertaken similar planning. A vital, and sometimes neglected, task is to make sure that the hard work of the teachers is celebrated. Recognizing and celebrating successful collaboration efforts helps teachers feel that their efforts are worthwhile and makes success in future collaborative efforts more probable.[4]

It may be necessary to focus teachers on the need to spend the time and effort necessary for planning activities. Group-building activities can be used to highlight the need for such planning. An example of such a group builder follows.

## Group Builder: Teacher

*Objectives:*   1. Teachers will identify synonyms for the word "teacher."
2. Teachers will recognize other opinions about teachers.
3. Teachers will experience success in working in groups with other teachers.

*Materials:*   Writing materials for each group

*Procedure:*   Teachers are grouped in heterogeneous groups of three or four. The leader gives each group five minutes to write as many synonyms for the word "teacher" as possible. One teacher in each group is appointed to write down the group's answers. The synonyms must be in English and must be single words. Hyphenated words are acceptable.

Some possible responses: leader, guide, facilitator, mentor, professor, helper, coach, rabbi, guru, truth teller, trainer, educator, lecturer, schoolmaster, instructor.

At the end of the time, each group shares a word from its list. This can continue until no group has any synonyms that have not been shared by other groups. If negative synonyms are mentioned, make note of them. If not, share some from the following list: Gestapo, blabberer, guard, stifler, trivialist, labeler, warden, discourager, jailer, grader.

Give each group five minutes to discuss what kind of students might agree with the negative labels for teachers. What would their reasons be? Have teachers share examples of those among their current students who might be likely to have negative images of the teacher.

*Individual Accountability:* Each teacher writes or shares with the group an idea for a way to improve the negative feelings some students have about teachers.


## PROBLEM SOLVING

Groups of teachers can be highly effective in developing strategies to address specific problem areas in the school. Problems may be specific, such as graffiti in the bathroom, or general, such as lack of school spirit. As with other interactive efforts, the group must feel comfortable in working together, and the specific skills needed for success in group work must be taught as needed.

Problems may be identified by the administrator or by individual teachers or groups of teachers. A group of teachers who are interested in working with the problem can be designated by the administrator. It is important that a committee include every teacher interested: limiting the number of teachers is usually not desirable.

At first, teachers may be reluctant to volunteer to work as a member of a problem-solving group. It is reasonable to expect limited participation when first undertaking such activities, but usually some of the staff will be willing to serve. The administrator or teachers who have volunteered may be able to solicit participation by visiting individually with teachers who would be helpful to a particular group's effort. As further groups are formed, the administrator may find some teachers overcommitted; that is, they are volunteering for too many responsibilities. For some teachers, this is appropriate; they thrive on activity and participation. The administrator may need to counsel with other overinvolved teachers who may be in danger of burning out and suggest that they can be more effective working with fewer groups.

A common difficulty in forming problem-solving groups is the unwillingness of some staff members to volunteer to work on any group function. These are sometimes the same staff members who are highly critical of the product of the group's effort. These teachers can often be recruited by individual members of the group. An individual teacher who asks a colleague with whom he or she has a rapport to help out with a group task will usually meet with a more positive reception than will an administrator who undertakes the same task.

The group effort should begin with a charge from the administrator that explains the function of the group and the reason the group was created. The charge should help the group organize its efforts. The most important task of the charge is to define the problem or area the group will be studying. This definition comes from the problem as it was identified. Defining the problem helps the group narrow its efforts and avoid unproductive tangents.

One of the first tasks of the group will be to determine a desired time line for its efforts. When will the group be meeting? When is the recommendation of the group needed? The administrator may want to meet with the group to assist in formulating a workable time line and to facilitate meeting time and location if such help is needed.

During the charge to the group, it is sometimes helpful to suggest that the group first focus on generating ideas that may serve as solutions to the problem. At this stage of the group's work, the leader will want to encourage the group to use strategies such as brainstorming to come up with ideas. The ideas should not be evaluated at this stage. Often, groups spend too little time at this stage of the process. In their legitimate desire to solve the problem, groups sometimes fail to consider many different possibilities and ideas.

An important consideration during the early work of a group is the desired outcome(s) of its efforts. What behavior or attitudes does the group desire to effect? How will the group know that change has taken place? What data or observation will be considered as evidence of the successful change?

When the group is satisfied it has generated a sufficient number of ideas, the leader may suggest that the group take the ideas to the faculty as a whole for input. This input can be encouraged in small groups that discuss the ideas the group has brought to them and comment on each one. The problem-solving group can then meet again and consider the faculty's input.

At this stage, the group will want to formulate goals or plans for implementing one of the ideas. A time line needs to be developed if the implementation should be completed by a certain date. During the charge, the administrator will want to caution the group not to try to implement too many ideas at one time. It is usually advisable to concentrate on one or two strategies at a time.

The final product of the group is usually a recommendation, in the form of a suggested action plan, for the implementation of the strategy that the group feels will be useful in helping to solve the given problem. This recommendation can be accepted or modified by the administrator and then presented to the faculty as a whole.

After providing the charge to the committee and assisting in the development of the time line, the administrator should encourage the group to develop its own strategies for attacking the problem. Each group should be encouraged to be creative and willing to look beyond traditional structures and solutions. The following group-building activity assists teachers in identifying different ways to solve a given problem.

## Group Builder: Fifty Percent

*Objectives*:
1. Teachers will identify different ways to solve a problem.
2. Teachers will recognize the value of collaboration in finding different solutions to problems.
3. Teachers will experience success in working on a group activity.

*Materials*: Writing materials for each teacher

*Procedure*: At the beginning of this activity, teachers are not grouped. The teachers are given two minutes to work individually on the following task: "Write 50 percent as many different ways as you can." Any solution that equals fifty percent is acceptable.

At the end of the activity, teachers are grouped heterogeneously in groups of three or four. Each group counts the total number of different responses from all members of the group. Each group then looks for the following different ways to solve the problem: using words, using numbers, using pictures, using foreign language words. Other solutions group members may have located are also identified.

Each group then reports to the whole group, telling how many different responses and ways of problem solving were found. The leader then shares William Glasser's assertion that in classes of eighth grade or beyond, fifty percent of the students are probably not putting forth the needed ef-

49

fort to learn to their potential. Small groups then discuss this assertion. Is this true of their students? What percentage of students are not actively involved in learning?

*Individual Accountability:* Each teacher writes down the names of students in a given class or classes whom he or she believes are not putting forth effort to learn and submits the list to the administrator.

Note: Administrators may wish to consider how teachers would interpret the intent of this part of the activity before implementing it.

*Follow-Up Activity:* Various group-building activities such as Success for All Students below may be used as follow-up group-building activities.

The administrator should monitor the progress of the group and assist as needed by providing materials, ideas from other schools, and clerical assistance from the school office. The school secretary can be useful in typing minutes, notes, and ideas from meetings to keep all group members informed. For example, after the following group-building activity, a list of all ideas generated by the staff could be typed and distributed by the secretary.

## Group Builder: Success for All Students

*Objectives:* 1. Teachers will identify ways in which they help students achieve success.
2. Teachers will identify ideas from other teachers that might be useful for their own students.
3. Teachers will experience success in a group-building activity.

*Materials:* Writing materials for each group
Lists of ideas from other groups
Recording chart for follow-up (Figure 4–3) (optional)

*Procedure:* Teachers are grouped in heterogeneous groups of three or four. One teacher is appointed in each group to record the group's ideas. Each group is given 10 to 15 minutes to generate as many ideas as its members can for helping students experience success. These may be ideas group members use in their own classrooms, ideas they have heard about, or new ideas that the group creates. Any idea is acceptable and should be recorded.

50

## Figure 4-3
### Recording Chart for Success for All Students Group Builder

Use some of the suggestions given to make each student in your class feel successful at least three times during one week. Use the seating chart to fill in each student's name, and then make a tally mark each day he or she has an opportunity for success. Each student should have three marks by Friday.

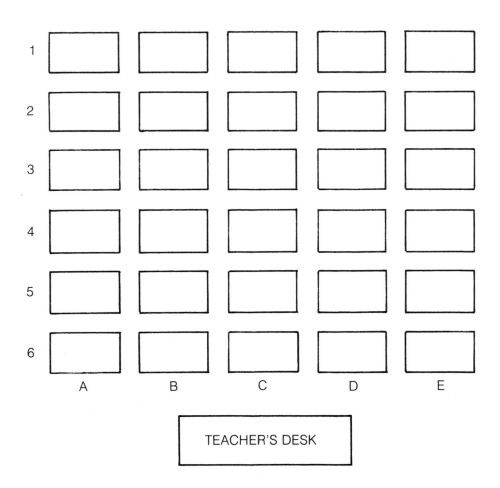

At the end of the thinking process, each group is given a copy of ideas generated by other groups. The list in Figure 4–4 was generated as a result of using this activity with several groups of teachers. Each group is then given five to ten minutes to compare its members' ideas with the ones on the sheet. The task is to note ideas the group members thought of that are not represented on the idea sheet they have been given. This is done by placing a check mark by the idea they think is different. If they are not sure whether their idea is the same, they should note it.

After the groups have compared their ideas with the idea sheet, each group shares with the whole group ideas its members came up with that were different from the ones on the idea sheet. The leader should stress that it is all right if the group did not think of any different ideas. The leader should also stress that if the group is not sure whether its idea is the same as one on the idea sheet, the idea should be shared. Each group should be given the chance to share only one idea at a time. The leader should go around to all groups at least once to encourage them to share any ideas. Groups that have many ideas can share in turn until their ideas are exhausted. The completed list is given to the leader who has the secretary type and distribute the list.

*Individual Accountability:* Teachers can be given a copy of the recording chart to use with one of their classes. On the chart, the teacher records the names of all students in the class. Each time an idea from the list is used with a student, the teacher puts a mark by his or her name on the chart. The goal is to give each student three (or more, if the administrator chooses) success opportunities in a week's time.

*Follow-Up Activity:* At a future meeting, teachers share experiences they had with using the success ideas with their students.

At times, the group may call on the administrator to help resolve conflicts or deal with impasse situations. Shared decision making requires that the administrator resist the urge to take control of the group and manage the dilemma. If the administrator offers solutions too quickly, the group may perceive that the administrator is not really committed to sharing the decision. Interference in the group's process, therefore, should take place with extreme care.

While conflict and impasse are uncomfortable for adults, teacher groups can usually work through these situations successfully. This is one of the strengths of shared decision making: when more people have in-

## Figure 4-4
## List of Ways to Make Students Feel Successful
## for Success for All Students Group Builder

1. Have high expectations for every student.
2. Use appropriate touches and physical contact.
3. Actively listen to students.
4. Individualize learning experiences for students.
5. Use materials and activities that complement student learning styles.
6. Talk to students with respect and courtesy.
7. Provide meaningful, sincere praise.
8. Point out positive student accomplishments.
9. Give positive reinforcement.
10. Give students the chance to answer a question correctly.
11. Display student work in the classroom or hallway.
12. Provide learning activities on an appropriate level for each student.
13. Write a positive note or make a positive phone call to parents.
14. Let students help other students learn something.
15. Make a positive comment about each student's work.
16. Let each student tell the teacher or class something of importance to the student.
17. Let each student run an errand, be a monitor, or do a classroom job.
18. Let students show new students around the school.
19. Let each student be the class "star" for the week or day.
20. "Catch 'em being good."
21. Say each student's name.
22. Compliment each student about something.
23. Make other students aware of a student's accomplishments.
24. Use success cards/happy-grams/up slips/warm fuzzies/stickers.
25. Maintain direct eye contact with students.
26. Allow students to choose appropriate parts of their learning.
27. Encourage peer support for students.
28. Attend extracurricular activities.
29. Notice and comment on improvements students make.
30. Encourage students to compete against themselves.

put into a decision, more factors are considered and more solutions suggested. When positive ideas come from conflict, conflict becomes growth-provoking and affirming.

One of the frustrations in working with groups is that volunteering for a group seems to commit the teacher to an endless process of meetings. It is important that when the group has finished its task, the successful effort be celebrated and the group disbanded. Should further work be needed, a new group can be formed that can utilize the input of the previous group and that may include members of the previous group.

While some long-standing groups are perhaps useful, specific, task-oriented groups working together for a clearly defined purpose are often more productive and less stressful for the participants. One of the most important functions of the administrator is to serve as a barometer of the faculty to measure when too many groups are meeting and too many ideas are being tried. Lasting change is not accomplished quickly.

Another kind of problem-solving group is being used to discuss the needs of students who are not performing well in class. These student-advocate teams are made up of classroom teachers, special education personnel, support teachers, counselors, and other professionals who know about the child involved. Parents are sometimes a part of these teams as well.

The student-advocate team has the task of analyzing the student's performance to try to recommend strategies for making the student more successful in school. The student-advocate team considers test data, teacher observations, records of behavior, attendance, health records, and other information to make personalized recommendations appropriate to the needs of the particular student. The team sometimes recommends further evaluation by psychologists or social workers.[5]

Group building can be used to help all teachers feel more positive about working with students who have difficulties. Such students can be disruptive and discouraging to teachers who try to work with them, and support and understanding from other teachers are helpful. Since many of the students who are troubling a certain teacher will be passed on to other teachers in future years, working together as a team is essential for student success. The following group-building activity helps teachers see the perspective of the student who may need extra help to succeed.

## Group Builder: My Teacher Doesn't Understand Me

*Objectives*:
1. Teachers will analyze a poem and discuss the feelings of the student portrayed in the poem.
2. Teachers will relate the poem to students they know who have difficulty in school.
3. Teachers will experience success working on a group activity with other teachers.

*Materials*:
A copy of the poem "My Teacher Doesn't Understand Me" and the discussion questions for each group (see Figure 4–5)
A copy of the poem for each teacher after the activity is completed

*Procedure*:
Teachers are grouped in heterogeneous groups of three or four. Each group is given a copy of the poem and the discussion questions. One person in the group is appointed to read the poem to the group. Another group member is assigned to write responses to the questions. After 10 or 15 minutes, groups share their answers with the large group. Each teacher is given a copy of the poem at the conclusion of the exercise.

*Individual Accountability*:
Each teacher shares with the small group or writes an idea for showing students who have difficulty that teachers are sympathetic and caring.

## HELPING NEW TEACHERS AND STUDENTS

Teachers can help relieve the anxiety and isolation that accompany being new in the school. For the new teacher, returning teachers can serve as a support group to help that teacher get acquainted, identify resources, learn policies, and become an active participant in the school. The administrator could ask for groups of three or four teachers who would be willing to work together to help a new teacher become comfortable in the school. This would ideally be done a semester before the group is to work with the new teacher.

Successful interaction between the new teacher and the support group can take place only when the group has been adequately trained for its task and when group building has taken place. Groups that volunteer to work with the new teacher should be willing to spend some time working together to become effective in their task. The school district may wish to consider compensation for the effort the group is making.

When orientation groups have been identified and approved by the

## Figure 4-5
## My Teacher Doesn't Understand Me

I really want to learn to read,
But it is hard to follow the lines,
When the words jump around,
It makes the symbols look like signs.

I wish my teacher would understand.

Writing a lesson paper,
Is really hard for me.
I know what the answer is,
But I can't put it down for my teacher to see.

I wish my teacher could understand.

When I walk across the room,
Desks and chairs get in my way.
I can't seem to walk quietly.
I try to do better each day.

Why can't my teacher understand?

When will my teacher,
Learn about me?
Changing my assignments,
Would help me be me.

Someday my teacher will understand.

—Jo Anne Terrell[6]

### Discussion Questions

1. Why is the student in the poem frustrated? (Give at least three reasons.)

2. How could the student's teacher be more responsive to his or her needs?

3. What is the *tone* of the poem?

4. Do you have students like the one in the poem?

administrator, a planning session should be conducted to determine the desired activities for new teachers. These may include a tour of the school, a tour of the district's media center, and introductions to personnel in the school. The group may want to sponsor a faculty get-together for the new teachers. The administrator can be helpful in making sure that school efforts do not unproductively overlap orientation programs already in place at the district level.

In addition to initial activities to acquaint the new teacher with the school, groups may take the responsibility for orienting the new teacher to the district curriculum guides. The group may also explain the testing programs of the district and any special programs at the school level. The administrator may find it desirable to provide a review session on the curriculum guides and testing program, or the curriculum director for the district may provide such training.

Orientation groups may also take responsibility for making sure the new teacher is comfortable in the first weeks and months of teaching by checking regularly with the teacher and providing assistance as needed. The following group-building activity may help orientation group members determine which members can be effective in different areas of the new teacher's orientation.

### Group Builder: Who Can Help?

*Objectives*:  1. Teachers will identify staff members with skills in particular areas.
2. Teachers will get positive recognition from their peers for their talents.
3. Teachers will experience success in working with other teachers in a group.

*Materials*:  A list of the kinds of assistance new teachers may need for each group (see Figure 4–6)

*Procedure*:  This activity should be done by all members of the staff, including those who may want to serve on orientation committees. Teachers are grouped heterogeneously in groups of three or four. Each group is given a list of the kinds of assistance new teachers may need. The group suggests faculty members who could help in each area. The group may suggest no more than three teachers for each area. A teacher may be used in more than one area. At least one teacher should be suggested for each area. The teachers suggested may or may not be serving on orientation groups.

57

When the lists are completed, each group submits its list to the principal who has the lists from each group collated and typed by the secretary. The lists are then distributed to teachers. Any teacher mentioned for a certain kind of assistance may have his or her name removed from the final list on request.

The final list is available for orientation groups to give to new teachers who may request help in certain areas. The orientation group may suggest members to help, whether or not they are on the list.

## Figure 4–6
## A Help List for New Teachers

Please list at least one current faculty member who could help a new teacher if requested in each of the following areas. You may include as many as three different teachers for each area.

1. Help with classroom organization
2. Help with discipline
3. Help with testing
4. Help with parent relations
5. Help with audiovisual equipment
6. Help with different ways to teach
7. Help with time management
8. Help with bulletin boards
9. Help with locating resources for teaching
10. Help with motivating difficult students
11. Help in referrals for special education
12. Help in joining teacher groups
13. Help in taking a university class or graduate program
14. Help with finding a preschool or day care center
15. Help with finding sports activities
16. Help with finding clubs or civic organizations
17. Help with finding churches in the community
18. Help with finding an exercise or aerobics group

*Note*: Other ideas may be added by each group or by the administrator.

An evaluation should be conducted after the first semester of each orientation group's work with each new teacher to determine the effectiveness of the efforts. Suggestions from the evaluations can be incorporated into future orientation activities.

Like new teachers, new students also come into the school anxious and isolated. Support groups similar to the new teacher orientation groups can be organized for new students at the classroom or school level. As students help other students become comfortable in their new school, their own self-esteem is enhanced.

An activity that some schools have found useful at the beginning of the year is a night for new students and parents to come to school. This is particularly effective when the activity takes place before the new school year begins. Activities for such a get-acquainted night might include a tour of the school, a review of the school rules and procedures, and an introduction to school personnel who are able to attend. Group-building activities to help students meet other new students can help to relieve the anxiety of being alone. As students find other newcomers to the school, friendships can be formed and isolation reduced.

## IMPROVING INSTRUCTIONAL SKILLS

Interaction between teachers can also result in the improvement of instructional skills. Peer coaching is a promising strategy that has been used with success in many schools. Experienced teachers can serve as mentors to new teachers, using many of the same skills as peer coaches. Teachers can also help student teachers gain proficiency in instruction during their student-teaching experiences.

Peer coaching requires specific training in order to be successful. Peer coaches and mentors should be able to identify specific instructional behaviors that are being used in the instructional episodes they observe and to label these behaviors accurately. Data collection must provide the peer coach or mentor with an accurate record of a classroom observation. The coach or mentor must be able to use this record to analyze the instruction and to plan for the conference.

Conferencing is a skill that requires practice. The coach or mentor must be able to give helpful information, assist the teacher in becoming self-analytical, and reinforce productive teaching behaviors that have taken place during the observation. The successful conference requires the same degree of planning as a successful classroom lesson.

Peer coaches and mentors can benefit from regular interaction with other peer coaches and mentors. This support group provides opportunities to share successes, discuss problems, and improve coaching skills.[7]

The skills required of the peer coach or mentor are also required of the teacher who serves as the supervisor of a student teacher. The student-teaching experience is the culmination of a prospective teacher's professional coursework and requires interaction with a supervisor who has the specific skills necessary to help a student teacher gain expertise and confidence.[8]

In addition to the training required for successful coaching and supervision, the coach, mentor, or supervisor must also be able to build rapport and trust with the teacher with whom he or she is working. Group-building activities can be used to help the coach, mentor, or supervisor and his or her teacher get acquainted and feel comfortable with each other.

Instructional improvement should be a frequent focus of the faculty meeting and staff development session. Groups of teachers should have regular opportunities to share strategies, discuss problems, and brainstorm ideas. Such interactions require group-building activities to help teachers trust each other enough to share openly in this important area.

### Group Builder: How Many Ways?

*Objectives*: 1. Teachers will identify different strategies for teaching a lesson.
2. Teachers will share ideas about different strategies they have used to teach lessons.
3. Teachers will experience success in working on a group activity.

*Materials*: Paper for each group
A list of teaching strategies (see Figure 4–7) (optional)

*Procedures*: Teachers are grouped in heterogeneous groups of three or four. They are then given five to ten minutes to think of as many different strategies as they can for teaching a lesson.

At the conclusion of the first part of the activity, each group is given a list of different strategies for teaching a lesson. The groups are then given five to ten minutes to compare their group lists with the given list. Each group then shares with the whole group any ways its members thought of to teach a lesson that were not on the given list.

## CONCLUSION

Teacher interaction can have productive results if barriers of time, unfamiliarity, and distrust are broken down. In order to restructure the school to facilitate teacher interaction, administrators and teachers will have to find creative ways to overcome these obstacles.

Teachers can help to plan for the changes that restructuring will bring to the school. Their input can make sure that improvements have the support of the teaching staff and that strengths of the school are recognized and maintained as changes take place.

Teacher interaction can also be useful in solving problems. Teacher groups, created as needs arise, can work together to find creative answers to problems. The administrator is crucial to the success of problem-solving groups.

## Figure 4-7
## 30 Possible Teaching Strategies

| | |
|---|---|
| 1. Active listening | 16. Lecture |
| 2. Audiovisual, television | 17. Music, drama, fine arts |
| 3. Chalkboard work | 18. Peer tutoring |
| 4. Coaching | 19. Physical activity |
| 5. Computer assisted | 20. Practical experiences |
| 6. Cooperative learning | 21. Programmed instruction |
| 7. Demonstration | 22. Projects |
| 8. Discovery | 23. Question and answer |
| 9. Drill | 24. Research |
| 10. Field trips | 25. Role playing |
| 11. Games | 26. Seatwork, homework |
| 12. Guided practice | 27. Simulations |
| 13. Guest experts | 28. Small group discussion |
| 14. Laboratory experiences | 29. Tests |
| 15. Learning contracts | 30. Trial and error |

*Source*: Lawrence Lyman, Alfred Wilson, Kent Garhart, Max Heim, and Wynona Winn, *Clinical Instruction and Supervision for Accountability*, 2d ed. (Dubuque, Iowa: Kendall/Hunt Publishing Co., 1987).[9] Reprinted with permission.

Teachers can also work as members of student-advocate teams to assure that all students receive an appropriate educational experience. The collective experience and insight of teachers meeting to devise strategies for students who are not succeeding are necessary if the growing number of at-risk students is to be significantly reduced.

Because the school experience often causes anxiety and feelings of isolation for new teachers and students, veteran staff members can be a positive influence on newcomers to the school. When orientation programs for newcomers are based on small-group interaction, positive attitudes toward the school are nurtured, and isolation and anxiety are reduced.

A significant area in which teacher interaction is crucial is the area of instructional improvement. By serving as peer coaches, mentors, and student teachers' supervisors, teachers can make a contribution to the professional growth of their current and future colleagues. Such interaction also enhances the instructional skills of the coach, mentor, or supervisor.

All of these efforts to promote teacher interaction rely on training. Teachers do not necessarily bring the needed skills to work effectively as members of groups in the situations described in this chapter. Specific training and skill building are needed to assure success and enhance the productivity of groups.

Group building is also necessary to create positive relationships among teachers who will be asked to function as members of teams. As group-building activities build rapport and understanding among teachers, they will be better prepared to work together. Group-building efforts increase the probability that teacher interactions will produce positive results.

If schools are to be restructured, teacher interactions with their colleagues will be a key factor in facilitating change, building positive attitudes, and increasing student achievement. As teachers work as members of small groups and teams, they will learn they are not alone in their task. Schools cannot be effectively restructured without the active participation of the teachers in them. Positive change requires that interactions among teachers be increased and be made more beneficial and rewarding for all.

## NOTES

1. A comprehensive examination of the conditions under which teachers work and the implication of these conditions for school improvement can be found in Ann Lieberman and Lynne Miller, *Teachers, Their World, and Their Work* (Alexandria, Va.: Association for Supervision and Curriculum Development, 1984).

2. A discussion of goal setting and the teacher can be found in Lawrence Lyman et al., *Clinical Instruction and Supervision for Accountability*, 2d ed. (Dubuque, Iowa: Kendall/Hunt Publishing Co., 1987), 22–25.

3. Some practical considerations for setting goals are offered in Tom Peters, *Thriving on Chaos: Handbook for a Management Revolution* (New York: Knopf, 1987), 270–71, 498–500, 512–15.

4. Peters (see note 3) also discusses the importance of recognizing and celebrating accomplishments in *Thriving on Chaos*, 307–12.

5. One model for student-advocate teams is described in David R. Riel et al., "Intervention Assistance Teams: Collegial Decision Making to Help Faltering Students," *ERS Spectrum* 7, no. 4 (Fall 1989): 17–21. The advantages of peer collaboration in helping classroom teachers and special education teachers work together are discussed in Marleen C. Pugach and Lawrence J. Johnson, "Facilitating Consultation Through Peer Collaboration," *PAISE Reporter* (Pennsylvania Resources and Information Center for Special Education) 21, no. 1 (October 1989): 1–2.

6. Jo Anne Terrell is a special education teacher in the Geary County Unified School District, Junction City, Kansas.

7. Support groups and other suggestions for a successful peer-coaching program are offered in *Clinical Instruction and Supervision for Accountability* (see note 2), Chapter 10. Setting up a school-based model for peer coaching is described in Lawrence Lyman and Michael Morehead, "Peer Coaching: Strategies and Concerns," *Thrust for Educational Leadership* (California Association of School Administrators) 17, no. 3 (November–December 1987): 8–9.

8. The role of the classroom teacher as student teacher supervisor is discussed in Michael Morehead, Lawrence Lyman, and Scott Waters, "A Model for Improving Student Teaching Supervision," *Action in Teacher Education* 10, no. 1 (Spring 1988): 39–42.

9. Another good resource describing many different teaching strategies with appropriate references is Sharon Zenger and Weldon Zenger, *Basic Ways to Teach: in the 80's*, (Saratoga, Calif.: R and E Publishers, 1985).

# 5. POSITIVE INTERACTION AMONG YOUNGER STUDENTS

From the moment a student enters school, he or she must learn to participate in group activities and interact socially with other students who may be very different. As students grow older, their elementary classrooms often become teacher-oriented, and student learning becomes individual and isolated. Teachers who use interactive learning approaches recognize that perhaps the most important learning resources are frequently neglected in this traditional classroom. Traditional classrooms focus on teachers, books, and other materials as the sources for learning. In interactive learning classrooms, however, student interaction becomes the most important learning tool in the classroom, making more productive use of teachers and learning materials.

Teachers who use interactive learning approaches recognize the often underutilized potential of promoting active student interaction in the learning process. The interactive classroom uses cooperative learning processes as a primary learning method in the classroom. Many other small-group and individual strategies complement the cooperative methods and assure that different student learning styles are accommodated.

Interactive learning classrooms use a series of methodologies such as cooperative learning that, used together in a well-planned system, have been shown to increase student achievement, improve student self-esteem, improve student understanding and retention of material, and enhance the student's desire to learn, now and throughout the student's life.

## CLASSROOM ENVIRONMENT

In the interactive classroom, the environment consists of cooperatively made goals, democratic structure, and group problem solving when concerns occur. Conflict provides opportunities for further learning, rather than frustrating teacher and students. The students become accountable, not only as individuals, but as members of the group as well. At the heart of the interactive learning classroom is an atmosphere of caring that is nurturing and supportive for each student.

## AWARENESS OF OTHERS

Throughout their preschool and elementary school experiences, students become aware of students who are different than they are. Positive interaction with these different students helps all students to appreciate and value each member of their class. Individual differences, cultures, and ideas can then be celebrated.

## SELF-ESTEEM

Student self-esteem is promoted as students interact positively with each other. Positive interaction produces support for each member of the class. Individuals are valued and can honestly feel that the class is less productive and powerful if they are not present.

## COMMUNICATION

Interaction during the learning process provides frequent opportunities for oral language experiences for students. Cognitive oral rehearsal during interaction improves the students' understanding and retention of what is being learned. Important skills for communicating with others are also practiced and enhanced.

## CREATIVE / CRITICAL THINKING

Creative thinking and critical thinking are emphasized in the interactive classroom. Brainstorming, innovation, synthesis, problem solving, application, and analysis become the end goals of student learning experiences, rather than rote memorization and repetition of established ideas and patterns.

## SAMPLE GROUP BUILDERS

Teachers do not have to rebuild the classroom to provide these interactive opportunities for student success. Teachers can continue to use their same materials and instructional objectives. By restructuring the classroom to promote positive student interaction, teachers can meet students' cognitive needs and their affective needs as well.

Younger students do not bring the skills needed for successful group interaction to their early school experiences. If successful interaction is to take place in preschool and elementary classrooms, group builders must be used. These activities provide positive experiences for students in working with others and opportunities to practice interaction skills.

Teachers can use group builders to begin the restructuring of their classrooms so that the outcomes of the interactive classroom can be realized. The following group builders provide examples of activities targeted to each of the outcome areas: classroom environment, awareness of others, self-esteem, communication, and creative/critical thinking.

## Group Builder (Environment)
## Vanity License Plates

*Objectives*:
1. Given various vanity license plate statements, students will attempt to determine what those license plates are trying to communicate to others.
2. Students will create a vanity license plate that communicates a positive idea about something members of their group have in common.
3. Students will experience success in working on a group activity.

*Materials*:
No special materials required, other than the handout (see Figure 5–1) and a pen or pencil

*Procedure*:
Give each group of three students one Vanity License Plates handout. You should have one student be a writer who fills in the handout as the group decides on the correct responses. One student should be the leader so that someone guides the discussion. One student should be the reporter. When the students have finished the activity, the reporter writes the group's vanity license plate on the chalkboard for all students to see. You should have the class guess what the vanity license plate stands for and what the group is attempting to communicate with that license plate.

## Group Builder (Awareness of Others):
## Group Bulletin Board

*Objectives*:
1. Given a variety of materials, students will make a bulletin board collage that represents their understanding of themselves as human beings.
2. Given a knowledge of themselves as human beings, students will find and cut out letters, words, pictures, advertisements, and other items that represent their personal likes and dislikes, feelings, emotions, thoughts, or situations.
3. Students will experience success in a group activity.

66

## Figure 5–1
## Vanity License Plates

Match the owner with the GR8 license PL8s below. As a group, think of a vanity license plate of your own to share with the class.

1. YDRYV55   4. 2 DALOO   7. UPN ATM

2. GDAY M8   5. HOME RN   8. IN XTC

3. 2TH DR    6. NOV L T   9. AW SHUX

10. H8 2 LUZ

_____ Little Abner

_____ A baseball fan

_____ A travel agent'

_____ A Crocodile Dundee fan

_____ A 55-mph speed limit opponent

_____ A dentist

_____ A very competitive person

_____ An inventor

_____ A very happy person

_____ A morning person

*Follow-Up:*    Each group should think of a license plate that could describe the group, e.g., LV2READ, SKATERS, FTBL FANS. Completed license plates are to be displayed in the classroom.

---

*Materials:*    Magazines, newspapers, and journals collected from home or from the school librarian prior to discarding
Construction paper, poster board
Glue, tape, or adhesive

*Procedure:*    You will tell groups of students to discuss the idea of what makes a person a human being as compared to any other animal on earth. Students might respond with the ideas of feelings, emotions, thoughts, and likes/dislikes. Write the ideas on the chalkboard. If students do not suggest the previous ideas, add them to the list.

Now have the groups of students make a collage by cutting out various parts of magazines or newspapers and gluing them to the construction paper or poster board.

Place these collages on your bulletin board. Have the groups of students share what the collages mean in regard to each student.

## Group Builder (Self-Esteem): Who Is It?

*Objectives:*
1. Given a drawing that represents each student's face, the student will see how other students view him/her.
2. Given a drawing that represents each student's face, the student will hear positive statements about his/her features.
3. Students will experience success in a group.

*Materials:*
Pencil or crayons
Paper

*Procedure:*
Students should be placed in groups of three. Each group is given three pieces of paper and pencils or crayons. Each student writes his or her name on the back of a piece of paper. Then each student chooses a part of the face to draw on all three pieces of paper. Student #1 may draw the shape of each student's head on each piece of paper. Student #2 may draw each student's chin on the face. Student #3 may draw each student's nose on the face. This continues until the group members feel that their faces are represented on each piece of paper.

The pictures are placed on a bulletin board or held up for the class to view. Class members can guess whom each face represents. However, before students guess who it is, they must say something positive about the person as viewed in the picture. For example, "This person has pretty eyes. I think it is Mary." Negative comments should be discouraged.

The students' pictures can be handed back to each student so that names may be written below the faces. These pictures can be put on the bulletin board. This group builder can be done at the beginning of the year in order to help classmates learn each other's names.

# Group Builder (Communication):
## Working for Peanuts

*Objectives:*    1. Given a drawing of an elephant and construction paper peanuts, pairs of students will practice
   a. their counting skills by counting out peanuts and placing them on the elephant.
   b. their spatial relationship vocabulary words by putting the peanuts on or off and above or below the elephant.
2. Given a drawing of an elephant and construction paper peanuts, pairs of students will communicate with each other and assist each other in a positive helping manner.
3. Students will experience success in a group activity.

*Materials:*    A drawing of an elephant (see Figure 5–2)
Five "peanuts" made out of construction paper (During the activity, each pair of students should have only one drawing of the elephant and five peanuts to share. Each child may later be given an elephant to color, if desired by the teacher.)

*Procedure #1:*    You should tell students that they will be working in pairs to feed the elephant and that you will tell them how many peanuts to give the elephant each time they feed it. Students will take turns feeding the elephant by putting peanuts on the drawing. One student puts the peanuts on the elephant drawing and the other student checks to see that the correct number of peanuts is properly placed on the elephant drawing as directed by the teacher. For example, you may say "Put one peanut on the elephant's stomach." One student carries out the direction, and the other student checks to see that one peanut is on the elephant's stomach. You may choose to use the following number format:
1. one peanut
2. three peanuts
3. two peanuts
4. no peanuts (State that the elephant is not feeling well or that the elephant is full right now.)
5. five peanuts
6. four peanuts

*Procedure #2:*    To practice spatial relationship vocabulary words and counting at the same time, you may say "Now you will use the correct number of peanuts and place the peanuts where I ask you to place them." You may wish to use the following format:

69

Figure 5–2
An Elephant Working for Peanuts

1. one peanut on the elephant
2. two peanuts off the elephant (in the blank space outside the drawing of the elephant)
3. one peanut on and one peanut off the elephant
4. two peanuts on and two peanuts off
5. three peanuts on and one peanut off
6. two peanuts on and three peanuts off

Changing the order of the "on" and "off" location words, you might state

7. three peanuts off and one peanut on the elephant
8. four peanuts off and one peanut on
9. one peanut off and no peanuts on
10. no peanuts off and two peanuts on

You could substitute the words "above" and "below" or "left" and "right" for "on" and "off." Example: one peanut above and one peanut below the elephant (in the blank space outside the drawing of the elephant). A group reward could be peanuts or peanut butter cookies.

## Group Builder (Creative Thinking)
## Cooperative Pumpkins

*Objectives:*   1. Given the drawing of a pumpkin, students will
    a. practice cutting skills.
    b. identify body parts (eyes, nose, mouth).
    c. cooperatively design a Halloween pumpkin.
 2. Given the drawing of a pumpkin, three students will design and make a creative face for the pumpkin by sharing the drawing of the face together
 3. Students will experience success in a group activity.

*Materials:*   A pumpkin drawing (see Figure 5–3)
Crayons or magic markers
Scissors
Paste
String

*Procedure:*   You should group students into threes. Each group is given a drawing of the pumpkin. You should assign each student in the group a number (1, 2, and 3).

Student #1 begins cutting out the pumpkin. After a short interval of time, Student #2 should have a turn cutting out the pumpkin. Student #3 should cut along the dotted lines. All students in the group should have approximately the same amount of time to cut.

Student #1 should take the top of the pumpkin (with the stem). This student is responsible for putting eyes on and

71

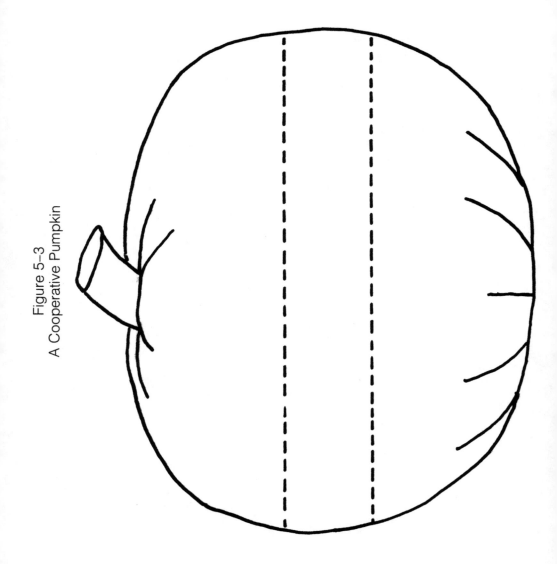

Figure 5–3
A Cooperative Pumpkin

decorating this part of the pumpkin.

Student #2 should take the middle part of the pumpkin. This student is responsible for putting the nose on and decorating this part of the pumpkin.

Student #3 should take the bottom part of the pumpkin. This student is responsible for putting a mouth on and decorating this part of the pumpkin.

After students finish their parts of the pumpkin, have them put the parts together and see how their pumpkin face turned out. You may want to have students take their pieces of the pumpkin to other groups and make whole new pumpkins. The completed pumpkins can be displayed on a bulletin board or hung from the ceiling as a mobile. (Paste one group's pumpkin parts on the back of another group's pumpkin parts and link them together with a string.)

Group Builder (Critical Thinking):
A Science Experiment

*Objectives:*
1. Given a class discussion about the forces of the reentry and landing process of astronauts, students will hypothesize about the effects of landing on earth with adequate and inadequate protection.
2. Given the class discussion and hypothesizing about the effects of landing on earth, students will make their own protective landing crafts for a raw egg in order to enjoy a cooperative effort and build the excitement of wonder about the anticipated success or failure of their landing craft.
3. Students will experience success in a group activity.

*Materials:*
Raw eggs
Various containers of the students' own choosing
Tape, string, and other adhesives
Crayons, paints, and other decorative materials
Space Travel handout (see Figure 5–4)

*Procedures:*
*Before the Experiment.* Tell students about astronauts and the forces that affect them upon entering the earth's atmosphere and landing on the earth. This could be done in conjunction with a space program takeoff and landing.

Have the small groups of four students hypothesize using question #1 on the Space Travel handout. When students have finished this section, explain about the science project. Students are to design, decorate, and fly/land their spacecraft in order to keep an egg from breaking. Do not state whether the egg is to be raw or hard-boiled only that they will be using an egg instead of a real astronaut. Students will assume that you mean a raw egg.

After the explanation about making landing crafts for the eggs ("astronauts"), have the groups of students complete question #2 on the handout. Have students hypothesize about whether the eggs will break or not. Have them also hypothesize about whether they can design and build a landing craft that will keep an egg from breaking.

Once the groups have finished hypothesizing about the project, have them list three things to do that would ensure the safety of the egg "astronaut" when landing on the ground. Have them use question #3 on the handout to write out their responses.

*During the Experiment.* You should next have students design, decorate, and build a landing craft for their egg "astronauts." After each group's landing craft is built, students should reread their responses to question #2 and state in question #4 whether the landing craft will now protect their "astronauts." Students need to explain their answers.

You should now take students outside, perhaps during recess, in order to conduct the experiment. This avoids cleaning up any mess that might occur if the experiment were conducted inside the building.

The class should decide how far the landing craft should travel in terms of feet. Students should also decide how far the landing craft should drop to earth.

Each group should then take turns launching and landing its egg "astronaut." This should be a "fun" time for the students.

*After the Experiment.* You may wish to launch and land your own landing craft. Obtain a small sandwich container that has locking edges. Hard boil an egg, and put it into the container. Do not tell students that it is hard-boiled. Allow the egg to roll around in the container. Have students hypothesize what will happen to your egg. They should guess that there will be a mess or that "yuck" will happen. Then launch and land your hard-boiled egg. Since it did not splatter (being hard-boiled), ask students to hypothesize why your egg did not break, get runny, or splatter. Some students will claim you tricked them. But some students might have thought to hard boil their eggs and call it a special spacesuit that protects the egg "astronaut."

This experiment will help students think about the launch and reentry of spacecraft, but also it will provide an entertaining and creative way to drive home the point that space travel is a complex and difficult activity.

## Figure 5–4
## Space Travel:
## Launching and Landing Spacecrafts

Facilitator _____ Encourager _____

Writer _____ Reporter _____

Choose a group role. The facilitator helps the group decide how to answer each item. The writer puts each answer on the paper after the facilitator says it is ready to be written down. The encourager makes positive comments to each student and about the task. The reporter will tell the class about the group's answers and discussion when the teacher requests that information.

1. What factors can affect a spacecraft's reentry into the earth's atmosphere and its landing on earth?

2. Do this question after the teacher has explained the experiment. What do you predict will happen to the egg "astronaut"? Why do you think this will happen?

3. What could be done to design a "spaceship" or landing craft that would protect the egg "astronaut" when landing on the ground? Think of at least three things you could do.

4. Reread your answer to question #2 above. Now that you have completed a landing craft, do you think that your egg "astronaut" can land safely in it or not?

*Follow-Up*:  Individual students can design their own landing crafts for their egg "astronauts." These can be launched to determine if individual students were successful in landing the "astronauts" safely. An added interest builder might include the use of raw eggs instead of hard-boiled eggs.

75

# 6. POSITIVE INTERACTION AMONG OLDER STUDENTS

As students leave elementary school, the environment in which they attend school changes. Often classes in middle schools and high schools isolate students. Participation in learning activities often declines, with some researchers estimating that only half of the students attending school beyond the eighth grade are active participants in their education.

When teachers use interactive learning methods, the roles of the teacher and student are different. The teacher acts not as a disciplinarian and teller of truths but as a facilitator or manager, so that students find and develop their own knowledge—knowledge that leads to long-term learning.

## CLASSROOM ENVIRONMENT

As older students continue to use the interactive skills they learn in the lower grades, the classroom environment changes from one of isolation to one of caring and support. Although building a classroom environment that promotes positive interaction is more difficult if students are inexperienced in interactive learning, group building and skill instruction can help students interact successively.

## AWARENESS OF OTHERS

In an interactive classroom, students are very involved in cooperative group processes, social support systems, cooperative learning, brainstorming, and shared classroom management decisions. The teacher helps the students learn to function together as a cohesive group. The students and the teacher can then work together for positive outcomes. This is particularly important when students change classes and see many different instructors and students during a school day.

To adolescents, positive peer relationships are tremendously important. Many adolescents do not have opportunities to build such relationships outside of school and are unskilled in social interaction. Many potentially likable students are labeled as different and undesirable because other students do not have enough opportunities to get to know them. In classrooms that promote interaction among students, students have an opportunity to get to know other students and develop positive relationships with them. Those who are "different" can often be perceived more favorably.

## SELF-ESTEEM

As students move from class to class in a middle or high school, they can easily become lonely and isolated. This alienation is particularly acute when the student has difficulty in forming social relationships. When students feel no one cares about them, self-esteem declines. This decline in self-esteem can result in dropping out of school, mentally or physically. Students may then seek to build their self-esteem through experimentation with drugs or sex.

The interactive classroom promotes positive student self-esteem by providing a support group for the student. This support group helps the student to succeed in learning activities and encourages active participation in learning. Student interaction can also produce feelings of positive self-worth and group membership that in turn increase liking of self, of peers, of adults, and of school.

## COMMUNICATION

Classrooms in middle schools and high schools are often silent places where students study in isolation. Interactions are limited to dialogues between the teacher and a few bright, verbal students. Many students have little opportunity to practice and improve their communication skills in such a classroom. In interactive classrooms, students are actively involved in communicating with each other. Written group products become more important, and each student has a stake in making sure the writing accurately reflects the group option.

Group roles can be useful in making sure that each student has opportunities to practice different communication skills. For example, a student can be the group's recorder one day, practicing listening and writing skills. Another day, the same student can be the group's facilitator, responsible for leading the group.

One of the most desirable benefits of interaction for older students is that interaction requires active listening to others. Such listening is an essential skill for academic and nonacademic settings beyond the classroom.

## CREATIVE/CRITICAL THINKING

Because information and technology are expanding at an incredible rate, traditional reliance on memorization and repetition of established patterns and ideas will not suffice for the secondary students of the 1990s. World problems of ecology, economics, and politics will challenge future graduates to be able to analyze information, apply learnings to specific situations and problems, and solve problems. Students will also be required to be creative through brainstorming ideas, synthesizing, and producing innovative ideas.

As students interact in small groups, they can gain a respect for the ideas of others. By interacting with others, students can learn different strategies and approaches to problem solving and appreciate divergent thinking. New and creative approaches are encouraged and celebrated in such a setting.

Time is a factor in planning learning activities for older students. Often, the teacher is limited to a specific time period each day. Understandably, many teachers are reluctant to "waste" precious classroom time on student interaction. One of the most consistent findings about cooperative learning, however, is that student achievement can increase even though initial investments of time are required. As students are more motivated to work and as they feel a part of their class, attention and work habits improve. Interactive learning actually makes better use of valuable student and teacher time.

## SAMPLE GROUP BUILDERS

Group building is necessary to set the stage for positive interaction among older students. To save some time, group builders can be used as short activities at the beginning or end of class. For older students, group builders offer opportunities to get to know fellow students, to become involved in the classroom, and to practice skills needed for successful interaction in other learning activities. Group builders can be positive "add-ons" to the schedule for the secondary teacher concerned with the morale and achievement of students.

Group Builder (Environment)<br>
Alike and Different

The teacher group builder Alike and Different can be adapted for student use. This activity would help promote a positive interactive environment in the classroom.

*Objectives:*     1. Given the flower handout, Alike and Different, the students in groups of four will find that there are similarities and differences among themselves as well as among the class.

78

2. Given the activity, students will be provided the basis for friendly interaction that helps build a positive environment within a small group and within the classroom.
3. Students will experience success in a group activity with other students.

*Materials:*    Alike and Different handout (see Figure 6–1)

*Procedure:*    Divide the class into groups of four. Within the center of the flower, students should list at least ten things that they have in common within their group. For example, each member of the group may be wearing eyeglasses.

In each of the four petals of the flower, students should write their own name. In each named petal, students should then list at least two things that make them different from the other members of the group.

When the handout is completed, you should ask each group to pick one item from the center of the flower that the members think no other group wrote down as a commonality within the group.

You should then ask each group for its unique commonality. Determine if other groups had this one in their ten commonalities. You could give 3 points to the group if no other group had its item, 2 points if only one group had the item, and 1 point if several groups had the item.

Select a group or two to share any unique items that individuals may have written in the outer circles.

You should feel free to enjoy this session with the students. Several choices may be humorous and fun for students. Students should be made aware of the many individuals in the classroom who have things in common with others. This makes each student aware of the others around the classroom.

Figure 6–1
Alike and Different

## Group Builder (Self-Esteem):
## Sharing Positive Feelings

*Objectives:*
1. Students will share positive feelings about themselves and others with other students.
2. Positive student feelings about the school will be displayed in the room.
3. Students will experience success in a group activity.

*Materials:*
A sheet of paper for each group to record ideas
A list of incomplete statements for each group (See Figure 6–2)

*Procedure:*
Students are grouped in heterogeneous groups of three or four. In each group, a student is appointed to read the list of incomplete statements. After each statement is read, each group member completes the statement with something that is true about him or her. It is not necessary to provide much time for discussion of the positive statements. The goal is for each group member to share something positive. When the last item is read, each group is asked to appoint a recorder to write down the ideas that are stated in the group. Each group member is accountable for having one idea written down on the group sheet, but ideas are turned in anonymously. The teacher makes a copy of all group responses, combining where appropriate if he or she chooses. The completed responses are displayed on a chart or bulletin board in the classroom.

## Figure 6–2
## Statements for Sharing Positive Feelings

1. One reason you're lucky to have me in this class is
2. Something I really like about school is
3. I know I've really helped another student when
4. Something I'm really proud of is
5. One thing I tried that worked out well was
6. A teacher makes my day when he/she
7. One of the best things about my classes this semester is
8. I like the principal because
9. This has been a good day (week) because
10. Something I'm really looking forward to is
11. One thing our class does really well is

# Group Builder (Awareness of Others):
## Autograph Party

*Objectives:*
    1. Given the autograph activity sheet, students will begin to know information about each class member.
    2. Given the autograph activity sheet, students will become aware of the fact they they are very similar to and yet different from their classmates.
    3. Students will experience success in a group activity.

*Materials:*
    An Autograph Party activity sheet for each student (see Figure 6–3)

*Procedures:*
    You will give each student one of the Autograph Party activity sheets. Each student will obtain the signature of another student where the statement indicates something about that student.

    When all the spaces are filled, you will place students in groups of four. The four students in a group will discuss and then count the number of items that every member of the group has in common with other persons who signed their sheets. The total number can be counted for the group. Divide the total number to get a group average. See which groups have the most things in common by recording the group averages on the chalkboard. Then discuss with the students how wonderful it is to have a class in which they have so many things in common with each other.

## Figure 6–3
## Autograph Party

| | |
|---|---|
| Is in Scouts or 4-H | Is on a sports team |
| Has a hobby collecting something | Has a pet |
| Has a brother | Has a sister |
| Has attended school in another town | Has always lived here |
| Has been to a zoo | Went to another state |
| Is wearing blue jeans | Is wearing tennis shoes |
| Has six or more letters in 1st name | Has a nickname |

(A student may autograph this sheet only once.)

## Group Builder (Communication):
## Colorful Language

*Objectives:*
1. Given the concept that writing should be colorful and expressive in order to communicate well, students will practice the use of expressive language and then apply expressive language in a sports setting.
2. Given the activity, students will have a feeling of enjoyment when communicating through the use of expressive language.
3. Students will experience success in a group activity.

*Materials:*
Colorful Language handout (see Figure 6–4)

*Procedure:*
You should tell students that good writers use colorful, expressive language. This process keeps the writing lively, interesting, and motivating. Student groups should match the expressive words and then come up with their own colorful words. Have groups share their answers after Part A is completed. This will usually show students that more than one expressive word can be used. Then have students complete Part B. After this part is completed, have groups share their choices of expressive words.


## Group Builder (Creative Thinking):
## Five Definite Don'ts

*Objectives:*
1. Given several seemingly disparate phrases, students will find what these terms have in common as things one would definitely not do.
2. Given the activity, student groups will create their own version of Five Definite Don'ts and have the class guess the commonality of the phrases.
3. Students will experience success in a group activity.

*Materials:*
None required

*Procedure:*
The teacher will write the following phrases on the chalkboard:

Overcoats
Shyness
Shoes and socks
Dogs
Loud radios and television sets

# Figure 6-4
## Colorful Language

Good writers use colorful, expressive language to interest readers in their stories. For example, a sportswriter might write that the Dallas Cowboys were stampeded by a team they lost to in a football game.

*Part A*

Match these verbs to the appropriate team: deviled, dethroned, stalled, extinguished, dulled, scuttled, dirtied, tangled, shrunk, tamed, sunk, eclipsed, bucked, handcuffed, grounded.

In their recent loss,

1. the Detroit Lions were _____.

2. the Kansas City Kings were _____.

3. the Seattle Mariners were _____.

4. the Denver Broncos were _____.

5. the Tampa Bay Buccaneers were _____.

6. the Pittsburgh Steelers were _____.

7. the Phoenix Suns were _____.

8. the Chicago White Sox were _____.

9. the New York Jets were _____.

10. the San Francisco Giants were _____.

11. the New Orleans Saints were _____.

12. the New Jersey Nets were _____.

13. the Buffalo Sabres were _____.

14. the Calgary Flames were _____.

15. the San Diego Chargers were _____.

*Part B*

As a group, what colorful, expressive verb describes the loss of the following college teams.

1. The Florida Gators were _____.

2. The Emporia State Hornets were _____.

3. The Georgia Bulldogs were _____.

## Figure 6-4 (*Continued*)

4. The Eastern Kentucky Colonels were_____.

5. The Indiana State Sycamores were_____.

6. The Lehigh Engineers were_____.

7. The Oregon State Beavers were_____.

8. The Massachusetts Minutemen were_____.

9. The Idaho Vandals were_____.

10. The Delaware Fightin' Blue Hens were_____.

The teacher states, "What would you definitely not do with these five items? In other words, what do these have in common with one another?"

After the groups of students have attempted to find the commonality and are having a difficult time, a hint might be given: "Think about vacations." Other hints may be given if the student groups are struggling. The answer is "things you definitely don't take to the beach in the summertime."

Once students have quit groaning and moaning about your phrases, have them come up with their own Five Definite Don'ts. When the groups have created their own items, have them put the phrases on the chalkboard and allow other groups to guess the commonality of the phrases.

### Group Builder (Critical Thinking): STAR

*Objectives:*
1. Given their general knowledge and background, students will be able to recall, identify, and categorize two items beginning with each letter found in the word "STAR."
2. Given this activity, students will have a positive, successful experience that should make the class more enjoyable for students.
3. Students will experience success in a group activity.

*Materials:* STAR activity handout (see Figure 6-5)

*Procedure:* You should give one STAR activity handout to each group of students. Each group should choose someone to write the responses on the handout. Students should come up with at least two items for each category related to the letters in the word STAR.

# Figure 6-5
## STAR

Directions: In your group, write down at least two responses to fit each category, using the letters in the word STAR. Example:

| Types of Transportation | Ships | Trains | Airplanes | Race cars |
|---|---|---|---|---|
| | S | T | A | R |

Cities in the U.S.

Names of Sports Teams

Foods and Drinks

Characters in Books

Mammals

Things You Like About
School

# 7. ASSESSING THE OUTCOMES

Assessing the outcomes of the interactive process is a very important task. This assessment is different from the normal pattern of classroom evaluation. In the traditional classroom, the teacher does all or most of the evaluation process. In the interactive classroom, students become a crucial part of the assessment process. In addition, a supervisor who observes an interactive classroom or cooperative learning classroom must examine different aspects other than those in a traditional classroom.[1]

There are two levels of accountability: individual and group. Each student is held accountable for individual achievement, often expressed in individual tests or written papers. Each group is held accountable for group achievement, often in the form of a group evaluation sheet or group product. The teacher might function as an external observer and record the specific observation of individual groups on a written sheet. Group builders might be assessed using the following instruments.

## INDIVIDUAL ASSESSMENT

After the group has concluded its task, individual students might take a quiz or test to determine the level of individual retention. In addition, the handout that follows (Figure 7–1) can be used for assessment of an individual's work in the group-building process.

## GROUP ASSESSMENT

Group assessment can be accomplished by allowing each group to evaluate how the group functioned during the group-building activity. The members of the group can discuss how each member functioned during the group process and then by consensus assess the participation of each member. This small-group observation form might have student roles and names on it along with the expectations of the members during the group-building process. The Small-Group Observation Sheet (see Figure 7–2) is an example of a group assessment form. This sheet can be completed by the teacher as the teacher monitors the progress of each group. The teacher might have the group compare the teacher's observation with the group's consensus about its activity. The teacher can use the group's observation form, the individual assessment form, and the teacher's observation form to assess the involvement of individuals in the group-building process.

## Figure 7-1
## Individual Assessment Form

Directions: Circle the number that indicates your feelings about how well the group worked on the activity.

Not at all = 1  A little = 2  Some = 3  Quite a bit = 4  Thoroughly = 5

1. I helped our group decide how to work on the activity.   1  2  3  4  5

2. I helped all group members participate in the activity.   1  2  3  4  5

3. I made positive statements about the contributions of   1  2  3  4  5
others.

4. I asked questions of the group when I didn't under-   1  2  3  4  5
stand something.

5. I listened to others while they explained their ideas.   1  2  3  4  5


I could improve my working in the group by doing the following:

_____

_____

_____


An overall assessment of the classroom environment would help the teacher and students focus on how the class is structured. Students in groups can determine how each element of a classroom is developed, e.g., who makes the bulletin boards. The students check whether students make the decision, whether the teacher makes the decision, or whether a cooperative decision is made. Students can then become involved in the decision-making process in regard to homework assignments or other aspects of the class. The following activity—Who Decides?—can be used in small groups in order to assess the classroom environment.

## Figure 7–2
## Small-Group
## Observation Sheet

Class _____

Date _____

Period _____

| STUDENT NAMES | Speaks ideas | Listens to others | Participates in role | Helps others in group |
|---|---|---|---|---|
| FACILITATOR | | | | |
| RECORDER | | | | |
| MARKER | | | | |
| ENCOURAGER | | | | |
| CONTRIBUTOR | | | | |

## Who Decides?

Directions: Place a check mark under who decides how the activity is carried out.

| Activity | Students | Cooperatively | Teacher |
|---|---|---|---|
| 1. Makes classroom rules | ____ | ____ | ____ |
| 2. Plans daily schedule | ____ | ____ | ____ |
| 3. Plans activities | ____ | ____ | ____ |
| 4. Decides how learning will be demonstrated | ____ | ____ | ____ |
| 5. Makes bulletin boards | ____ | ____ | ____ |
| 6. Gives help | ____ | ____ | ____ |
| 7. Checks class papers | ____ | ____ | ____ |
| 8. Makes homework decisions | ____ | ____ | ____ |
| 9. Evaluates student progress | ____ | ____ | ____ |

*Your Plan:* When you have completed your group discussion assessing who decides how the classroom is operated, develop a plan of action that would increase your involvement in deciding how the classroom is operated in order to achieve educational objectives.

## CONCLUSION

Assessing the outcomes of interactive activities is a different process from the traditional pattern of only external teacher evaluation of students. The interactive classroom requires that students become a part of the assessment process in order to promote democratic principles, as well as ensure student attainment. In the restructured classroom, students are involved in planning, implementing, and assessing the outcomes of their learning abilities. Current classrooms do not need to be rebuilt along radically new lines; they do need to be restructured for interactive learning.

# NOTES

1. Dan Watson and Lyle Rangel describe the basics of evaluating cooperative learning in "Can Cooperative Learning Be Evaluated?" *The School Administrator* (June 1989): 8–10. Guidelines for instructional supervisors of cooperative learning classrooms are found in Elizabeth G. Cohen, *Designing Groupwork: Strategies for the Heterogeneous Classroom* (New York: Teachers College Press, 1986). A sourcebook containing a variety of assessment approaches that may be adapted to interactive learning is Blaine R. Worthen and James R. Sanders, *Educational Evaluation: Alternative Approaches and Practical Guidelines* (New York: Longman, 1987).

2. A variety of assessment checklists for homework can be found in Harvey C. Foyle, *Homework: A Practical Teacher's Guide* (Portland, Maine: J. Weston Walch, 1989).

# SOURCES FOR GROUP-BUILDING ACTIVITIES

Adams, James L. *Conceptual Blockbusting: A Guide to Better Ideas*. 3d ed. Reading, Mass.: Addison-Wesley, 1986.

Canfield, Jack, and Wells, Harold C. *100 Ways to Enhance Self-Concept in the Classroom*. Englewood Cliffs, N.J.: Prentice-Hall, 1976.

Chase, Larry. *The Other Side of the Report Card: A How-to-Do-It Program for Affective Education*. Glenview, Ill.: Scott, Foresman and Company, 1975.

Cihak, Mary K., and Jackson, Barbara Heron. *Games Children Should Play: Sequential Lessons for Teaching Communication Skills in Grades K-6*. Glenview, Ill.: Scott, Foresman and Co., 1980.

Fisher, Ken. *Isaac Asimov Presents Super Quiz IV*. New York: Dembner Books, 1989.

Foyle, Harvey C., and Lyman, Lawrence. *Cooperative Learning: Experiencing the Constitution in Action*. Bloomington, Ind.: ERIC Clearinghouse for Social Studies and Social Science Education, 1988. ED 293 791.

Fluegelman, Andrew, ed. *The New Games Book*. Garden City, N.J.: Doubleday, 1976.

Gibbs, Jeanne. *Tribes: A Process for Social Development and Cooperative Learning*. Santa Rosa, Calif.: Center Source Publications, 1987.

Johnson, Roger T., and Johnson, David W. *Cooperative Learning: Warm-Ups, Grouping Strategies, and Group Activities*. New Brighton, Minn.: Interaction Book Co., 1985.

Kreidler, William J. *Creative Conflict Resolution: More Than 200 Activities for Keeping Peace in the Classroom*. Glenview, Ill.: Scott, Foresman, 1984.

Lehr, Judy Brown, and Harris, Hazel Willis. *At-Risk, Low Achieving Students in the Classroom*. Washington, D.C.: National Education Association, 1988.

Levy, Nathan. *Stories to Stretch Minds*. Vol 1 and 2. 2d ed. New York: KAV Books, 1986.

Lyman, Lawrence, and Foyle, Harvey C. *Cooperative Learning in the Middle School*. Bloomington, Ind.: ERIC Clearinghouse on Reading and Communication Skills, Indiana University, 1989. Ed 302 866.

McLoone-Basta, Margo, and Siegel, Alice. *The Second Kids' World Almanac*. New York: Pharos Books, 1987.

Orlick, Terry. *The Cooperative Sports and Games Book*. New York: Pantheon, 1978.

Peterson, Patricia R. *The Know It All Resource Book for Kids*. Tucson, Ariz.: Zephyr Press, 1989.

Stanish, Bob. *Connecting Rainbows: Activities That Connect Self-Esteem, Values, Empathy, Cooperation, and Creativity*. Carthage, Ill.: Good Apple, Inc., 1982.

Stock, Gregory. *The Book of Questions*. New York: Workman, 1985.

von Oech, Roger. *A Whack on the Side of the Head: How to Unlock Your Mind for Innovation*. New York: Warner, 1983.

# SELECTED BIBLIOGRAPHY

Aronson, E. et al. *The Jigsaw Classroom*. Beverly Hills: Sage, 1978.

Cohen, E. *Designing Groupwork: Strategies for the Heterogeneous Classroom*. New York: Teachers College Press, 1986.

Deutsch, M. (1960). "The Effects of Cooperation and Competition Upon Group Process." In *Group Dynamics: Research and Theory*, 2d ed., ed. D. Cartwright and A. Zander. New York: Harper and Row, 1960.

DeVries, D.; Slavin, R.; Gennessey, G.; Edwards, K.; and Lombardo, N. *Teams-Games-Tournaments: The Team Learning Approach*. Englewood Cliffs, N.J.: Educational Technology, 1980.

Dishon, D., and O'Leary, P. *A Guidebook for Cooperative Learning: A Technique for Creating More Effective Schools*. Holmes Beach, Fla.: Learning Publications, Inc., 1984.

Foyle, H. C. *Homework: A Practical Teacher's Guide*. Portland, Maine: J. Weston Walch, Publisher, 1989.

Foyle, H. C., and Lyman, L. R. *The Interactive Classroom: Cooperative Learning*. 2 parts. Emporia, Kans.: The Teachers College, Emporia State University, 1989. Videotapes.

Glasser, W. *Control Theory in the Classroom*. New York: Harper and Row, 1986.

Graves, N., and Graves, T. "Creating a Cooperative Learning Environment: An Ecological Approach." In *Learning to Cooperate, Cooperating to Learn*, ed. R. Slavin et al. New York: Plenum Press, 1985.

Johnson, D., and Johnson, R. *A Meta-analysis of Cooperative, Competitive and Individualistic Goal Structures*. Hillsdale, N.J.: Lawrence Erlbaum, 1987.

_____. *Learning Together and Alone*. Englewood Cliffs, N.J.: Prentice-Hall, Inc., 1987.

_____. *Cooperation and Competition: Theory and Research*. Hillsdale, N.J.: Lawrence Erlbaum, 1988.

Johnson, D., Johnson, R., and Holubec, E. *Circles of Learning: Cooperation in the Classroom*. Rev. ed. Edina, Minn.: Interaction Book Company, 1987.

Joyce, B., and Weil, M. *Models of Teaching*. 2d ed. Englewood Cliffs, N.J.: Prentice-Hall, 1980.

Kagan, S. "Cooperation-Competition, Culture, and Structural Bias in Classrooms." In *Cooperation in Education*, S. Sharan, P. Hare, C. Webb, and R. Hertz-Lazarowitz, eds. Provo, Utah: Brigham Young University Press, 1980.

_____. *Cooperative Learning Resources for Teachers*. Riverside, Calif.: University of California, Riverside, 1989.

Kagan, S.; Zahn, L.; Widaman, K.; Schwarzwald, J.' and Tyrrell, G. "Classroom Structural Bias. In *Learning to Cooperate, Cooperating to Learn*, ed. R. Slavin et al. New York: Plenum, 1985.

Lyman, L. R.; Wilson, A. P.; Garhart, C. K.; Heim, M.O.; and Winn, W. O. *Clinical Instruction and Supervision for Accountability*. 2d ed. Dubuque, Iowa: Kendall/Hunt Publishing Co., 1987.

Schmuck, R.; Runkel, P.; Arends, J.; and Arends, R. *The Second Handbook of Organizational Development in Schools*. Palo Alto, Calif.: Mayfield, 1977.

Sharan, S. *Cooperative Learning in the Classroom: Research in Desegregated Schools*. Hillsdale, N.J.: Lawrence Erlbaum, 1984.

Sharan, S., and Sharan, Y. *Small-group Teaching*. Englewood Cliffs, N.J.: Educational Technology Publications, 1976.

Sharan, S.; Hare, P.; Webb, C.; and Hertz-Lazarowitz, R. eds. *Cooperation in Education*. Provo, Utah: Brigham Young University Press, 1980.

Sharan, S., and Hertz-Lazarowitz, R. "A Group Investigation Method of Cooperative Learning in the Classroom." In *Cooperation in Education*, S. Sharan, P. Hare, C. Webb, and R. Hertz-Lazarowitz, eds. Provo, Utah: Brigham Young University Press, 1980.

_____. "Classroom Social Climate, Self-Esteem and Locus of Control." In *Changing Schools: The Small-Group Learning Project in Israel*, S. Sharan and R. Hertz-Lazarowitz, eds. Tel-Aviv: Tel-Aviv University, 1981.

Sharan, S.; Raviv, S.; Kussell, P.; and Hertz-Lazarowitz, R. "Cooperative and Competitive Behavior." In *Cooperative Learning in the Classroom*, ed. S. Sharon. Hillsdale, N.J.: Lawrence Erlbaum Associates, 1984.

Sharan, S., and Shackar, H. *Language and Learning in the Cooperative Classroom*. New York: Springer-Verlag, 1988.

Sharan, Y., and Sharan, S. "Training Teachers for Cooperative Learning." *Educational Leadership* 45 (1987), 20–25.

Slavin, R. *Cooperative Learning*. Report no. 267. Baltimore, Md.: Johns Hopkins University, Center for Social Organization of Schools, 1978.

_____. *Using Team Learning: The Johns Hopkins Team Learning Project*. Rev. ed. Baltimore, Md.: Johns Hopkins University, Center for Social Organization of Schools, 1980.

_____. *Cooperative Learning: Student Teams.* 2d ed. Washington, D.C.: National Education Association, 1987.

_____. *Cooperative Learning.* New York: Longman, 1983.

_____. *Using Student Team Learning.* 3d ed. Baltimore, Md.: Johns Hopkins University, Center for Research on Elementary and Middle Schools, 1986.

_____. *Cooperative Learning: Theory, Research, and Practice.* Englewood Cliffs, N.J.: Prentice-Hall, 1990.

Slavin, R., and DeVries, D. " Learning in Teams." In *Educational Environments and Effects: Evaluation, Policy, and Productivity*, ed. H. Walberg. Berkeley, Calif.: McCutchan Publishing, 1979.

Slavin, R.; Sharan, S.; Kagan, S.; Lazarowitz, R.; Webb, C.; and Schmuck, R., eds. *Learning to Cooperate, Cooperating to Learn.* New York: Plenum Press, 1985.